Mentalization in the Family

Mentalization in the Family draws upon the latest research on child development, parenting, and mentalization theory to provide a comprehensive guidebook for parents, teachers, social workers, and any professional working with families today.

The book explains the core concepts of mentalization, an idea whereby an appreciation of internal mental states, both those of others and oneself, can lead to an understanding of overt behaviour. It explores key ideas central to this – such as attachment style, internal regulation, emotional compass, and parental navigation – but also offers practical guidance around issues such as play, siblings, boundaries, and sexuality.

Accessibly written throughout and featuring pedagogical tools that bring the theory into life, this wide-ranging book will be essential reading for a range of professionals, from those working with foster families to teachers working with troubled or disruptive children. It also offers a way for parents to better understand themselves, their own parenting style, and the dynamics which make up family life.

Janne Oestergaard Hagelquist is an authorized psychologist and accredited specialist in child psychology and supervision. She works with treatment, supervision, and training of professionals on topics such as mentalization, overcoming trauma, and PTSD handling.

Heino Rasmussen is organizationally trained and works with training and coaching on the implementation of the mentalization theory in organizations, teams, and families.

"Parenting and family life comes both completely naturally to us and yet is so complex at the same time, it can feel almost impossible to feel we've ever got it 'right'. In this wonderful book, Janne Oestergaard Hagelquist and Heino Rasmussen, both parents and clinicians make the impossible seem possible. Using clear language, wonderful images and providing us with a tool kit, they help us to regain our capacity to mentalize in the most non-mentalizing system of all – the family. This is the book you will wish your parents had read and which your own children will undoubtedly benefit from. I wish I had it before I had children!"

Sheila Redfern, Head of Service, Specialist Trauma and Maltreatment

"The authors use the mentalizing framework expertly to articulate for parents an understanding of child development that provides a basis for practical help in parenting. They have organized their presentation with crystal clarity while providing an abundance of everyday examples of parenting challenges accompanied by useful suggestions and strategies. Most importantly, they give primary weight to the quality of relationships among family members, grounded in sensitive and skillful mentalizing that the authors exemplify."

Jon G. Allen, PhD, Professor of Psychiatry in the Menninger Department of Psychiatry and Behavioral Sciences at the Baylor College of Medicine; and Senior Staff Psychologist in The Menninger Clinic, Houston, Texas

"In this new volume, Janne Oestergaard Hagelquist and Heino Rasmussen provide a sensitive and reflective guide for parents and families who wish to increase their mentalizing capacity. With humor and humility (two important characteristics of the mentalizing stance), and rich and vivid examples, the authors manage to gently convey not only the "what", but also the "how" of mentalizing. All parents and families can benefit from reading this book, and the volume also presents a very useful tool for psychoeducation that clinicians may use in their work with families."

Carla Sharp, PhD, Director of Clinical Training and the Developmental Psychopathology Lab at Houston University, Texas

Mentalization in the Family

A Guide for Professionals and Parents

Janne Oestergaard Hagelquist
and Heino Rasmussen

Routledge
Taylor & Francis Group

LONDON AND NEW YORK

Originally authored in Danish language by Janne Oestergaard Hagelquist and Heino Rasmussen with the original title *Mentalisering i familien*; © 2017 by Hans Reitzels Forlag, a division of Gyldendal publishing group, Copenhagen, Denmark.

Translated from the Danish by Heino Rasmussen.

First published 2021
by Routledge
2 Park Square, Milton Park, Abingdon, Oxon, OX14 4RN

and by Routledge
52 Vanderbilt Avenue, New York, NY 10017

Routledge is an imprint of the Taylor & Francis Group, an informa business

Library of Congress Cataloging-in-Publication Data
A catalog record for this book has been requested

ISBN: 9780367221010 (hbk)
ISBN: 9780367221027 (pbk)
ISBN: 9780429273230 (ebk)

Typeset in Bembo
by Apex CoVantage, LLC

Contents

Figures

Preface

The purpose of this book is to show how the theory and practice of mentalizing and the current knowledge of child development and parenting can be applied to support children's development in the best way possible.

The fact that we are parents ourselves makes it both easier and harder to write a book about child development and parenting. As parents and authors of this book we have learned that we have extensive experience and knowledge, while we, at the same time, feel incredibly humble towards the demanding task of parenthood – partly because we know that interaction with children is fast-paced and takes place in complex situations and partly because, as parents, we have our own ideas and feelings which inform our behaviour, so that we are not always able to act in accordance with the suggestions we make in this book. In our own everyday life, we are often confronted with doubt, mistakes, and feelings of inadequacy. In this book, we wanted to pass on information that has been helpful to us – knowledge about parenting we would have wanted to have when we first had children and knowledge that has helped us in our professional work with parents, foster carers, and professional caregivers.

Although we do not always do everything as well as we would wish, we still believe that knowledge about children and child development is important for the way we parent. We introduce the concept of mentalizing into the family because we find that it is extremely helpful for interacting with children. Mentalization and understanding of child development ensure that you do not rigidly fix upon a certain way of understanding your child. For instance, you might convince yourself that a 9-month-old child who does not want to be left in day care is bossy and difficult (if you are not familiar with separation anxiety, which manifests itself at this age). And when your teenager distances herself from her parents and puts all her energy into activities with friends, you might think that she is selfish, difficult, and misbehaved (if you are unfamiliar with the fact that breaking free from the family, bonding with friends, and experimenting with life are central developmental tasks for teenagers).

In this book, parents' own ability to mentalize is the primary tool. Mentalizing is the ability to look beyond behaviour, thereby gaining an understanding of what is happening in your own mind as well as in the child's mind. This requires an understanding of what your child is experiencing as well as of the child's developmental stage. In order to do this, it is necessary to build a relationship with the child, and practice looking at what lies behind your own behaviour as well as the child's, thereby gaining a better understanding of yourself and your child. When children interact with their parents, they develop the ability to mentalize on their own.

The book examines various concrete models and educational tools which can be helpful to foster carers, kindergarten teachers, and other professionals who work on developing and supporting parents. The book is just as useful for parents in their day-to-day job of supporting their children's development and learning.

We maintain that although spending time with children and as a family is about development and learning, it is primarily about understanding and using what parents are already able to do instinctively. We have attempted to create the same atmosphere in this book. We hope that the book will be a complement to the natural interaction between parents and child, which is playful, curious, and explorative. Use the models, be inspired by them, reflect on them as parents – but never let the models become more important than understanding the child.

Janne and Heino

Structure of the book

The book is divided into an Introduction and six practice-oriented chapters containing models and descriptions. The introduction presents the latest theory on child development, attachment, mentalizing, and parenting tools. The following is an outline of the six practice-oriented chapters.

Mentalizing – basic concepts

In Chapter 1, we examine various models of the basic concepts in the theory of mentalizing. The purpose of this chapter is to explain what mentalization means, what happens when mentalization fails, and the options that are available to the parent in terms of asserting authority and power when working with child development.

The nautical universe

In Chapter 2, we use the nautical universe as a metaphor for child development. The nautical universe offers a way of understanding parenthood which centres on the child's developmental process. The metaphor draws on sailing and sea voyages in its understanding of psychological development – and thereby better understanding the parent–child relation. This section also contains ideas and tools for parents to better support their child's developmental and learning processes.

The child's development

Chapter 3 contains a detailed examination of the child/the young person's development, divided into the following periods: 0–3 years, 4–8 years, 9–12 years, and 13–18 years. In each period, the child's development in six areas is presented in tables that are clear and easy to understand. The six central areas of the child's/the young person's development are as follows:

- Emotions
- Behaviour

- Physical development
- Relations
- Sense of self
- Attention/cognition

For each of these six areas, ideas on how to best support the child's development at each stage are presented. Additionally, at each stage, the state of development of mentalization is examined. This third chapter is intended as an index where parents can get an idea of whether the challenges their child is facing are normal developmental tasks that need to be supported and mentalized and how this can be done.

The mentalization toolbox

In Chapter 4, you are presented with a toolbox which contains tools for supporting development of appropriate behaviour. A lack of ability in another area can lead to inappropriate behaviour, which means that the desired behaviour cannot be learned before these aforementioned abilities have been acquired. For instance, the child must be able to recognize and regulate their own emotions before other abilities can be acquired. For this reason, the end of the section contains practical ideas for supporting the child's ability to register, categorize, verbalize, and regulate emotions.

The significance of childhood and the mentalizing family

In Chapter 5, we focus partly on the importance of the baggage parents bring into the parent–child relationship and their ability to take an observer's perspective of themselves as parents. Our approach to parenthood is coloured by our own history, upbringing, and baggage. In this section, helpful concepts such as angels, ghosts, triggers, and re-enactment in the nursery are outlined. And in part, this chapter presents ideas from research and structured family therapy on how to take an observer's perspective on one's family and how to structure one's family life in a way that creates the most optimal environment for mentalization for everyone in the family.

Challenges in parenting

In Chapter 6, we turn the spotlight on some special issues in parenting and development. Various models describe common challenges in parenting, and we make suggestions for how to understand and deal with them. It might, for example, be challenges regarding play, sleep, sexuality, siblings, lying, trauma, divorce, grief, and facing the empty nest when the grown-up teenager leaves home.

Reading guide

The diagram below can help you navigate the book and find the section and tables that are most relevant to you.

To make the models more accessible, they have been designed using the same template, which gives a good idea of the basis and possibilities for application of each model. To support this, every concept is structured around five headlines:

Introduction to topic/concept

We describe the topic/concept and its use in parenting and give a short introduction to the theoretical basis of the model.

Suggestions and strategies

We present our best suggestions and strategies on how to use the model, or if there are any pitfalls.

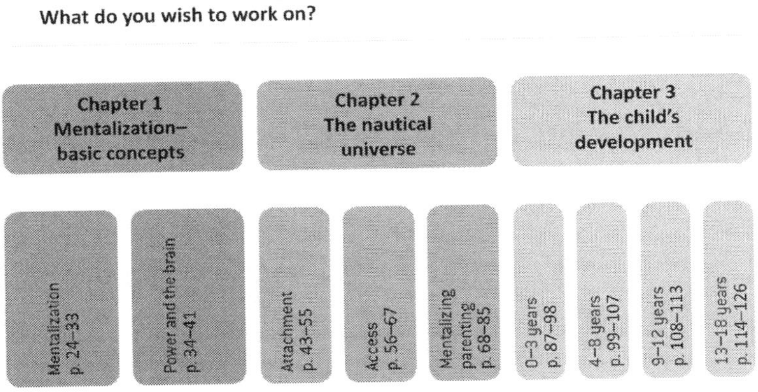

What do you wish to work on?

Chapter 1 Mentalization– basic concepts	Chapter 2 The nautical universe	Chapter 3 The child's development

Mentalization p. 24–33 | Power and the brain p. 34–41 | Attachment p. 43–55 | Access p. 56–67 | Mentalizing parenting p. 68–85 | 0–3 years p. 87–98 | 4–8 years p. 99–107 | 9–12 years p. 108–113 | 13–18 years p. 114–126

Figure 0.1 Reading guide

Example

The example is a small case-story which elaborates and puts a perspective on the uses of the model and its effects.

Model

The purpose of the model is to provide visual support for your understanding of the concept, help you remember it, and possibly make it easier for you to use it in practice.

How to do it?

After each model, we present some ideas for how to use the model in practice. Since this is not meant to be a rigid manual, the instruction is not rigid either, but rather is meant as an inspiration for how the model can be used.

Before you begin

No parent is perfect – and that is worth remembering before you start reading this book. Studies have shown that even the most sensitive of parents are not aware of what happens in their child's mind 50 percent of the time (Allen & Fonagy 2006: 87). The rest of the time they are talking to their partner and doing other things, such as cooking, looking after the child's siblings, or perhaps looking at their phone. So parents are not perfect – and they are not supposed to be. As long as they are good enough.

It is completely unrealistic to want to be perfect and respond all the time. In fact, by experiencing a lack of mirroring and feeling misunderstood, the child

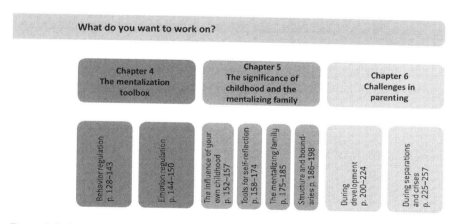

Figure 0.2 Reading guide (continued)

learns that other people have their own reasons for acting the way they do. The goal is not to be a parent who does not react to their child. This will happen automatically, but it is not helpful to you or your child if you always feel guilty when the child, for instance, is not heard immediately. By being flawed yourself, you also become a role model for your child, showing them that it is okay to make mistakes. Keep this in mind when you approach this book.

Introduction

The reflections on your own way of parenting and your child's mental states is the essence of *mentalization in parenting*. Simply browsing through a book like this is a form of mentalization.

When approaching child development through mentalization, you believe that from the time of birth onwards, children learn to understand their own mind by interacting with parents who are genuinely interested in understanding their child, their child's development, and the way their child experiences the world.

We attempt to summarize current knowledge of child development and how parents can support this development. The book can be viewed as a kind of replacement for all the knowledge that used to be passed on from generation to generation when we lived in extended families. We have attempted to explain, in a clear and straightforward manner, the most recent psychological knowledge on what constitutes good parenting and what it takes to develop mentally strong, well-functioning children who have a secure sense of self but who are also able to understand others.

The reason we have chosen the theory of mentalization as the framework for a book on parenting is that research has reliably shown that this approach has various positive effects on child development. We try to not overwhelm the reader with sources, but for the sake of the reader who wants to delve deeper into a topic, some references from the literature on mentalization are included.

The theory of mentalization

Mentalizing is described as a hallmark of emotional health and one's capacity for developing secure attachments throughout one's life (Allen et al. 2010). When parents mentalize in their interaction with their child, the child is able to develop their own ability to mentalize, as well as a secure attachment to their parents (Sadler et al. 2013; Fonagy 2008). Good mentalization facilitates the ability to register emotions, categorize, verbalize emotions, and regulate emotion (Allen & Fonagy 2006; Goldie 2004; Fonagy et al. 2007; Skårderud & Sommerfeldt 2014).

The concept of mentalization originates in psychoanalysis, and, since the early 1990s, the Hungarian-born psychologist Peter Fonagy and his colleagues have revitalized it, making it relevant and applicable for the everyday lives of children, young people, and their families. Mentalization can be defined in various ways. According to one definition, mentalization is the ability to focus on the mental processes of self and others, especially as a way of understanding behaviour (Bateman & Fonagy 2007: 33). Emotions, needs, goals, reasons, and thoughts are mental processes that influence behaviour. A shorter and easier way of defining mentalization is "keeping the mind in mind" (Allen et al. 2010: 26).

A well-developed mentalizing capacity helps us make sense of ourselves and our own behaviour, as well as the behaviour of others, and supports our capacity to see new possibilities and perspectives in relation to other people (Daubney & Bateman 2015). Parents' mentalizing capacity is connected to children's capacity for developing coherent understanding and meaning in their relation to and narratives of family and friends (Steele & Steele 2005). Thus, having a mother or father who keeps their child's mind in mind functions as a buffer for behavioural difficulties and disorders. This may owe to the fact that the child feels understood and consequently develops an interest in understanding others, which makes it easier for the child to respond to challenging social situations without having to resort to aggressive or negative behaviour (Hughes et al. 2017). In addition, the capacity for mentalization supports the child's ability to cope with challenging life situations – such as sexual abuse (Ensink et al. 2016) or living with a parent who has a substance abuse problem (Ostler et al. 2010).

We emphasize mentalization in our approach to child development – particularly children's emotional and social development. Parents tend to focus on emotional and social development only when they realize that their child has problems in these areas. But, as supported by the references mentioned, much would be gained by focusing on this part of the child's developmental process from the beginning, as it would lay the foundations for the child's emotional health.

The capacity for mentalization might be more important than ever before, because today's children are living in a complex world in which their life and relational challenges are unpredictable and demanding, much more so than in previous generations. In those days, when each generation grew up to follow in their parents' footsteps, people did not need the ability to adapt to different life situations. By contrast, a child born today must be flexible and able to cope with changes. By encouraging mentalization in the way they bring up their children, parents can support their children's ability to understand themselves and others in complex contexts. This encourages the child to be flexible and find meaning in their everyday lives as well as in new ideological universes. And these, we propose, are central abilities for the generation growing up today.

Example – teaching children to mentalize

The concept of mentalization and the related theory provide justification for what the good parent has always done but has not been able to put into words. Consider the following example:

Fifteen-year-old Simon is partaking in an exchange program at his school, and as part of the program, an Italian exchange student is coming to stay with Simon for a week. Two days before the exchange student's arrival, Simon's father tries to talk to Simon about his plans for the upcoming week. He approaches Simon just as he arrives home from school but hardly manages to ask before Simon proclaims that he couldn't care less about the "stupid Italian." Simon elaborates: "I'm never going to see him again anyway, after he's returned home." He looks tauntingly at his father, saying: "You are so afraid that your idyllic façade is going to crack. I honestly don't think I want to be here when he arrives – I'm just going to go out this weekend, while he is here, and get pissed."

After this tirade, he turns around, stomps down the hall, and slams the door to his room. The father is furious, and yells at Simon: "You are not going to get very far with that attitude!" In his room, Simon turns up the music and locks the door. The father thinks Simon is selfish and spoiled and feels like kicking in the door or calling Simon's teacher, telling her what Simon has said, and cancelling the visit. But the father is also familiar with mentalization and contemplates what is going on in his own mind at this moment. He is afraid that the Italian exchange student will have a bad experience (feelings). He wants to prepare for the visit (need), because he wants things to go well (goal), and perhaps it is himself, rather than Simon, who needs to prepare (reason). All of these aspects influence his behaviour as a parent.

He reassures himself by contemplating what goes on in Simon's mind. He recalls that Simon has an important soccer match this evening, and that he has been playing soccer matches most evenings this week. Simon seems stressed and under pressure (feelings); he usually does things one at a time (need), and it is hard for him to plan ahead, which means that he is always in the middle of things (reasons). Perhaps the reason why he does not want to talk about the exchange visit right now is that he is trying to protect himself so that he is able to deal with the upcoming match (goal).

The father decides to take care of all the preparations for the visit that he is able to on his side, if for nothing else then for his own sake. After the soccer match, he enters Simon's room to say goodnight, and finds his son crying under his blanket. Simon tells him that he feels under pressure from soccer, as well as being in the ninth grade, thinking about the upcoming exams, and now the visit from the Italian exchange student on top of everything. He tells his father that he wants the Italian boy to enjoy his stay, too.

In this example, it is helpful that the father focuses on the mental states of himself and Simon in order to understand why Simon behaves the way he does. The father has certain expectations of himself as a host and needs to make preparations, while Simon is only able to consider the next upcoming task. The father is aware that Simon's behaviour triggers intense emotions and the need to act in himself, and he chooses to actively use mentalization to regulate his own emotions. It turns out that he had an idea about the cause of Simon's behaviour, but that his son was actually under more pressure than he had imagined. The father is also aware that, although we can make assumptions about what is going on in the mind of our child, we can never know for sure. This is a central point in mentalizing.

When mentalization fails

Mentalizing parents behave as Simon's father did. From birth (even from pregnancy) onwards, they assume that their child has its own mind and that its actions are based on underlying intentions and treat them accordingly. Mentalizing parents are also characterized by being somewhat unrealistic about their child's ability to understand and act in the world, but in this positive field the child becomes an active agent. Mentalizing parents know that their child's mind can be difficult to comprehend from the outside, so they reflect on the possible reason for their child's behaviour and come up with several possibilities. In the example, Simon's behaviour might also be caused by him being unhappy in love or having fallen out with his best friend.

Mentalization is a dynamic capacity which is sensitive to stress and intense feelings. It is especially hard to continue mentalizing in relation to those people one has the strongest feelings for – typically one's children or one's partner.

When intense emotions lead to shifts in the brain which switch off the capacity for mentalization, we talk about mentalization failure. When this happens, you lose focus on your own and the other person's mental processes. You lose track of your own feelings, needs, goals, and reasons, as well as those of the other person. In the example, Simon suffers a mentalization failure, and his father nearly does, but by actively contemplating his own and Simon's mental states, he avoids it.

Everyone sometimes finds themselves in situations where they lose track of what happens in their own mind and in the minds of others. The circle below illustrates the way in which intense feelings can lead to mentalization failure, which leads to a higher risk of causing mentalization failure in others. In the example, Simon is frustrated with his father's demands, which he cannot cope with. As a consequence, he gets upset with his father without understanding his father and his father's feelings. Simon makes assumptions about his father only caring about façade. Simon acts on these assumptions by yelling at his father. But Simon's behaviour affects his father's feelings, which consequently also intensify, leading to poor mentalization in the father. On a less lucky day, Simon's father might have reacted by continuing in the vicious circle, but he becomes aware of the mentalization failure and manages to reintroduce mentalization into their interaction.

Mentalization is about being open and curious about your child's behaviour.

Rather than trying to control the behaviour, one must attempt to find meaning in it. One way of aiding mentalization – and stopping the need to act – is by adopting an open mind (represented by the Danish acronym "ÅBENT", meaning "open"). Essentially, this means trying to maintain an open mind about your own and your child's mental states. The open-mind approach is based on the following traits: openness ("**å**ben"), balance ("**b**alance"), empathy ("**e**mpati"), curiosity ("**n**ysgerrighed"), and patience ("**t**ålmodighed").

The open-mind approach arises from knowledge that you actually do not know what is going on in other people's minds, and consequently you must actively try to keep your own mind *open* to other possibilities instead of rigidly fixing on a certain way of thinking. In this respect, *balance* is central, because it is important to be able to find a balance between your own mind and what is happening in the other person's mind. Some parents are too focused on their

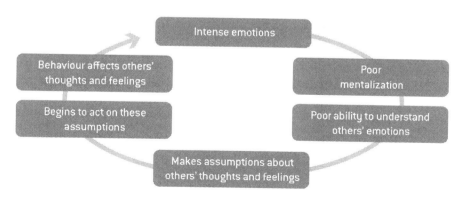

Figure 0.3 Illustration of mentalization failure

Source: Bateman & Fonagy 2012; Skårderud & Sommerfeldt 2014.

child's mind, while others are too occupied with their own minds. It is better to find a balance between the two – yet it is particularly important that the parent is able to find a balance in relation to their own mind, since they know more about the world and are able to take responsibility, and since they are the grown-up in the relationship, they must create a healthy and safe environment for the family. *Empathy* is the ability to recognize and understand other people's emotions. It is crucial for maintaining healthy, mutual interactions. *Curiosity* is important with regard to understanding the reason behind a certain behaviour. Consider the following questions: "Why does she hit her sister? Why does she cry at night? Why is he attracted to those boys? Why won't he play with my son?" These are essential questions in mentalization. *Patience* is the ability to accept that children's development moves slowly, and they do not always develop in the direction one hopes for – and despite that, one persists and continues to invest time and patience in the process.

We have now presented various reasons for the importance of the capacity for mentalization and have presented that mentalizing parenting is good and appropriate. The three most important reasons are as follows (Allen et. al. 2003):

1   Through mentalization, you get to know your own emotions, thoughts, and assumptions, and you learn to understand that they underlie your behaviour. It gives a sense of control over your actions, which, again, leads to a greater self-awareness and sense of identity.
2   Mentalization is the foundation for meaningful, lasting relationships. By mentalizing you see the other person's perspective, while at the same time you are able to be true to yourself in your relationships with others. This is the cornerstone of healthy relationships.
3   Mentalization is the key to self- and emotion regulation.

Learning, parenting, and parenthood

Out of all mammals, humans have the least developed brain at the time of birth; a human baby is incapable of taking care of itself and ensuring its own survival. Furthermore, humans are born into a complex social world, which means that, for the first 20 years of its life, the child needs to be in relationships where it has the opportunity to learn before it can become an independent part of the human species. The human child has to learn much more than other mammals, and consequently, it needs to acquire the essential social skills of language and mentalization.

The capacity for mentalization is developed in parallel with human evolution. As humans began creating tools, even tools that could create other tools, the world became increasingly complex. Language became an advantage, making it possible to teach the next generation about the world they were to be a part of. When humans introduced the division of labour, with some people specializing in different fields, it was advantageous to have a good understanding about what was going on in one's own mind as well as in the minds of others. This meant that the hunter could explain to the carpenter how his bow should be fashioned, and the carpenter could teach his child how to do woodwork and how to hunt. This development lies at the root of the capacity for mentalization.

In more advanced societies, it was necessary to establish social norms about how to interact with others, but this knowledge of culture, values, and norms was too advanced and specific to be passed on only through genes. It was necessary to have a group of people around the small child who could care for it and teach it how to interact with the complex world surrounding it. These attachment figures, typically the parents, provided a safe base from which the child could explore the world. Together with its parents, the small child could develop new skills and learn about itself and its body. It became aware of being a part of social relations and learned to understand itself and others. In short, it is the job of mentalizing parents to:

- Ensure the child's survival: caring for the child.
- Educate the child: supporting the child's understanding of the complex social world that it is part of, that is, norms, expectations about behaviour, rituals, and universes of meaning.
- Support the child's psychological development: developing the child's potentials, that is, its emotions, behaviour, physiology, relations, sense of self, cognition/attention, and mentalization (Fonagy et al. 2014).

When it comes to determining parental responsibilities, suggestions about what parents are responsible for are as numerous as there are parents and children. When we began writing this book, we asked 12-year-old Liva about her thoughts on good parenting. She gave the following answers on what parents ought to do:

- Not to be working too much.
- Make their children believe in the Easter bunny, Santa Claus, and the tooth fairy.
- Spend time with their children doing various activities.
- Help them with their homework.
- Encourage them to care about school.
- Make sure there are snacks available in the home so they won't go buy candy.

If you consider these statements, you can see that Liva actually knows that good parenting requires parents to be present, so that they can ensure their child's survival, and educate them, for example, on social norms.

Another girl, 9-year-old Clara, was asked to describe what it means to be a good father. She mentions the parental roles of supporting psychological development and learning, as well as caring for the child:

- Someone who comforts me when I am sad.
- Someone who helps me when things are difficult.

- Someone who is nice to me.
- Someone who doesn't leave me.
- Someone who loves me.
- Someone who helps me with my homework.
- Someone who cooks.

The most important responsibility for parents is to ensure their children's survival but also to teach the children how to survive on their own. In addition, children need to learn how to act in the social world that they are part of. They must learn everything. Everything from that it is okay to eat blueberries (but not berries from privet hedges) to knowing how to use the tools we surround ourselves with – from forks to computers. Their development must be supported in respect to a range of specific areas of development, which will be reviewed later in this book (see Chapter 4). In short, the essence of parenthood is to ensure the child's survival, teach the child how to behave in the culture they are part of, and encourage their psychological development, so that the child can realize their potential.

In many cultures, the word "discipline" is used in connection with parenthood. Discipline is Latin and means "to teach," so discipline has to do with educating one's children (Siegel & Bryson 2014). What is important is the task or responsibility. The obligation that parents have to teach their children everything that is not innate, so the child can become an independent adult. The most important task is teaching our children the things that ensure their survival and to avoid what is dangerous. In addition, our children must learn how to be a part of the social world surrounding them.

But in order to teach your child anything, you must be in a position where the child listens to you. Children are born to enter into learning relationships, but what mechanisms are required to maintain a relation where the child wants to learn from their parents? In other words, what are responsibility, authority, and power in relation to parenthood?

Responsibility, authority, power, and mentalization

In many ways, the parent–child relationship is an asymmetrical relation, as the responsibility, authority, and power lie with the parent. Responsibility, authority, and power are instruments for protecting the child, by defining, organizing, and set boundaries for the child. In return, interaction between parent and child enables the child to be a part of a vital, developmental interaction and offers the adult perspective and experience (Fonagy et al. 2014; Hafstad & Øvreeide 2011).

For biological parents, obtaining power and authority is basically unproblematic, since the child is predisposed to enter into relationships that ensures its survival and learning. The fact that power, authority, and responsibility lie with the parents have a range of advantages:

- The adult is stronger.
- The adult has the resources (money, food, security).
- Legally and culturally, the adult has been allocated responsibility, authority, and power over the child.
- Adults are smarter, and they can draw on experience and knowledge.
- The adult has a more mature mind and is regulated, accountable, and more mentalizing.

And yet the power relation is not inflexible. Power exists only through interaction and activity, and accordingly, between parents and child, power should be understood as a relational concept (Foucault 1994). Parents always hold the responsibility for managing this power for the good of the child and to support the child's development into an independent person who is eventually able to take charge of themselves and become a part of society.

Since birth, the child has an innate ability to assess the way in which its parents use power (Fonagy et al. 2014). The child has a natural (epistemic) hyperawareness when it comes to determining whether or not its educators are good, that is, whether its parents are able to use power properly and use it for the good of the child. This awareness ensures that the child pays attention to whether or not power is abused. A baby does not have many options when it comes to assessing and reacting, but it does have some, for instance if the parents do not fulfil their responsibilities. The child can shy away from eye contact and ultimately give up contact entirely, if the opportunity for learning available from its parents is not appropriate. As the child grows older, and in keeping with its physical and psychological development, more reactions are available to the child, such as avoiding or opposing its parents or seeking out other educators.

Clearly, it is important how parents address issues of power, authority, and responsibility. For instance, how does one assert one's authority as the child grows older, and the parents are, perhaps, no longer smarter, stronger, etc., than the child? Likewise, it is of great importance how you teach the child to use power and authority throughout its developmental process.

In the following, we review how different forms of power can be used in parenthood and what is most appropriate in the long run in different situations. Traditionally, power is divided into five different types of power, which parents naturally exercise over the child: punishment, reward, legitimacy, knowledge, and epistemic trust. In the original model on different forms of power, this was called reference power (French & Raven 1959), but the description shares many common features with the term epistemic trust from the mentalization theory.

These types of power can be considered in the same way that we view the diet pyramid, in which there should be more at the bottom and least at the top, but all parts should be included in parenthood. Up until now, we have placed power and authority side by side, but forms of power such as reward

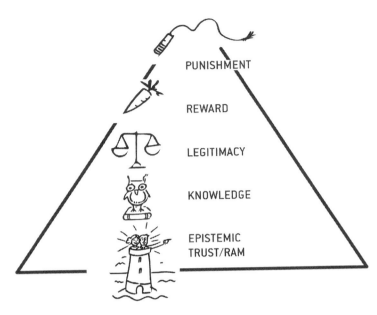

Figure 0.4 Illustration of the five types of power

Source: French & Raven 1959.

and punishment will often be found at the top of the pyramid, whereas those types of power that correspond to what we think of as authority are found at the bottom.

It can be helpful for parents to talk about the kinds of power one uses, and it is important to know that when you define this, you do it based on your own personal perspective. It is easy to imagine that the child would define the use of a certain form of power in a very different way. Parents might think that they use power based on knowledge when they say that their teenager cannot partake in parties arranged on Facebook which many young people attend who do not know each other. By contrast, the young person will most likely view this as a punishment. As mentalizing parents, it would be advisable to consider how the form of power appears from the child's perspective.

Punishment

Punishment is a broad concept, ranging from violence, confinement, and humiliation over loss of privileges and scolding to natural consequences. This is the traditional form of parenting. Some theorists suggest that this form of parenting stems from the days when humans started cultivating soil, and as a consequence developed a more hierarchical social structure. It was necessary to raise children to be a submissive, hard-working labourer, forming a natural part of the existing hierarchy (Gray 2013; Harari 2015).

Before we had legal systems, punishment was used to maintain law and order. When our ancestors kicked people out of the settlement it was a good thing for the survival of the group and served to maintain shared norms and values and ensure cooperation within the group. Therefore, it received positive feedback from other group members at the settlement. The fact that these actions had positive effects for the group as well as the individual is probably the reason why we react negatively when others do not respect common standards and why we feel relieved and satisfied when justice is done and order restored. This means that we have a capacity for experiencing physical pleasure when we punish – although of course this capacity is subject to individual differences.

This can be measured using brain scan technology, as those parts of the brain that react to pleasure will light up in brain scans when experimental subjects engage in acts of punishment (Quervain et al. 2004). This might explain the phenomenon known as a "sense of justice." When our sense of justice is violated it is experienced as an intense feeling, and that the offender should receive some sort of punishment is seen as appropriate and just.

This sense that justice needs to be restored is particularly appropriate for parenthood. For example, a mother living in France explains how she experiences disapproval from others because she does not discipline her son using corporal punishment. Sayings such as "revenge is sweet" or "he had it coming" refer to this human tendency to take pleasure in punishing others. Clearly, punishing behaviour that does not seem appropriate is probably part of human nature. The tendency to use punishment in parenting could, however, also have to do with parents feeling powerless in relation to their children, reminding us of feelings of inadequacy and helplessness in our own childhood. The consequence of feeling inadequate or powerless means that we lose the capacity for mentalization, and then punishment becomes the first tool we reach for.

In conflicts, parents might feel that their inner image of the child's mind is wiped out and exchanged with an empty or negative image (Fonagy & Allison 2014). When you have an empty or negative image of your child, punishment appears to be a reasonable strategy. Afterwards, you might justify it to yourself by telling yourself that punishment is the most reasonable way to support your child's development, such as: "Enough is enough"; "How else will he learn?"; "Should I just put up with her behaviour?"; or "If I hadn't punished him, he would have been spoiled, and no one would have been able to stand him."

Physical violence is one of the worst types of punishment. Violence has always been a part of parenting. For instance, in *The Common Sense Book of Baby and Child Care*, a classic in literature on childcare, the renowned American pediatrician Benjamin Spock wrote:

> I'm not particularly advocating spanking, but I think it is less poisonous than lengthy disapproval, because it clears the air, for parents and child. . . .

Moreover, I believe that it will do a child no harm to learn that it can make mother or father so angry that it has unpleasant physical consequences.

Today, we know that children from homes where there is violence have a wide range of developmental disorders and difficulties as a result, such as aggression, anxiety, depression, difficulties in conflict management, learning difficulties, and mentalization difficulties, as well as cognitive, social, and emotional difficulties (Bateman & Fonagy 2012; Hagelquist & Skov 2014). In the long term, then, violence is damaging to the child's development, but in fact it is also damaging in the short term, because it escalates the conflict. When violence is inflicted upon a child, or the child is physically restricted, its muscles tense, which releases adrenalin and makes him experience stress (Elvén & Wiman 2016). At the same time, violence shuts down the capacity for mentalization as well as other parts of the brain that are important for learning. The child's brain will, very appropriately, focus its energy to those of its centres dealing with fight, flight, or freeze (see the model on p. 40). When these systems are activated, there is less activity in the parts of the brain that deal with learning, and conflicts are more likely to escalate.

When parents – who are role models for their children – solve difficult conflicts by using power and violence, the child will imitate them and learn to use similar strategies. This means that there is a risk that the child, like their parents, will have a hard time dealing with conflicts with friends, and later with their partner.

> Eight-year-old Jamie keeps clashing with his friends at school. When the teachers try to talk to him about the conflicts, he "freaks out." As a consequence, even slight conflicts in school often result in Jamie being sent to the principal's office. Here, Jamie is also sometimes rude, and the conflict usually ends with the principal calling Jamie's father. Jamie is very scared of his father, and when he arrives Jamie turns silent, cowers in his chair, and does what he is told. Jamie's father does not understand why the adults around Jamie do not punish him harder – it works for him, and "Jamie knows what happens if he tries to act up with his father." The father does not realize that his strategy of punishment has left Jamie feeling powerless and without any constructive strategies for solving conflicts.

The example shows how Jamie is left unable to regulate himself and deal with conflicts. In Jamie's case, it is evident that he experiences a basic state of offence and hostility. This example should make it clear that violence is not part of good parenting.

There are other types of punishment more appropriate for parenting than violence, but these can also have negative side effects. The biggest problem is that punishment undermines trust, and trust is an important part of learning. It is central for parenting that the child trusts the person that attempts to teach them something. When the person who should be there to comfort the child or teach them how to regulate their emotions and to mentalize, even when it is hard, is also a source of anxiety and fear, the child loses their trust in that person. Since trust is the foundation for learning, this is very problematic. It is a good idea to keep the following quote in mind: "Never let correction sabotage for connection" (Larsen & Weele 2011: 94).

One type of punishment *is* appropriate for parenting, namely natural consequences. It is a form of punishment, but a mild one which ought to make sense to the child, while at the same time parents make it clear to the child that actions have consequences: "If you keeping losing your phone charger you will have to save money for a new one yourself," "If you won't put on your jacket you are going to be cold," "It might be a problem for you if you call your mother a cow, since cows can't give you pocket money."

Younger children are less able to learn from negative consequences (Elvén & Wiman 2016). For example, think about a small child who is just learning to walk and who repeatedly stands up just to fall down again. Fortunately, the child keeps attempting to walk rather than crawl despite such negative consequences. In general, small children learn very little from punishment. In fact, the child does not really learn from negative consequences and punishment until it is 11–15 years old. Small children are frequently unsuccessful, so it is normal for them to experience negative consequences, such as falling down. This does not lead to a great deal of learning, since we learn best when things deviate from what is normal. Fifteen-year-old children succeed more than they fail. Consequently, they are able to learn from negative consequences. Nevertheless, explaining to the child what it is doing well and when it has succeeded, is a better strategy. That way, the child learns more.

Reward

Parents have power over their children because they possess resources which the child desires, such as things, candy, money, or activities such as going to the cinema, playing board games, etc. In this context, we have decided to include praise as a reward, since praise and verbal support is something the child desires and can receive from its parents. Rewards can be of a tangible as well as a more social nature.

To parents, giving rewards can be a good way of gaining power, and all parents use rewards to some extent. If the rewards are tangible, such as things and activities, the rewards should be small and scaled down when the child has learned the behaviour. At this point, it is more appropriate to reward through praise, since there can be many drawbacks to using tangible rewards. First of all, it is a demanding and expensive solution, and second, there is a tendency for the rewarded behaviour to cease once it is no longer rewarded (Elvén &

Wiman 2016). In addition, if one uses tangible rewards it can easily turn into a negotiation and a sense of injustice because you have to spend energy on setting boundaries to avoid having to deliver more and bigger rewards.

Similarly, parents should take the time to consider how a given reward might be experienced by younger siblings:

> Six-year-old Ann is used to getting rewards, and when something is demanded of her, she always answers: "What do I get if I do it?" Eventually, her parents find it hard to motivate her to do as she is told, so they introduce a system where they use stickers as rewards for good behaviour. Ann's little sister becomes very resentful about it and demands to get stickers as well. But if she gets stickers too, Ann demands to have another kind of stickers. . .

This example illustrates the problem with only using tangible rewards. Initially, it might be used as a shortcut to motivate good behaviour, but eventually it can become a much more complicated and far greater mentalizing task than intended. Of course, this can be avoided by setting clear rules about when such rewards should be used, and small rewards can be good for learning new things. As a rule, however, helping each other should be something that one does without question in a mentalizing family.

Praise is a much better way of rewarding someone, but some forms of praise are more appropriate than others. Praise works best if it is specific and levelled at the individual child. It is the behaviour, not the child, that should be praised. This is known as "process praise." The following is an example of this type of praise: "I am very pleased that you put your plate in the dishwasher" rather than "You are so good." This type of praise supports the behaviour and the sense that you can improve yourself. Research has shown that children who receive process praise focus on strategies and hard work. When children find a task difficult, it is also important to focus on the process: "Let's talk about what you were trying to do just now, and what you can do better next time," or "That was really hard, but you made an effort" (Gunderson et al. 2013). However, it is possible to praise too much. It is better to give praise once in a while rather than all the time. But the worst is when children do not receive any praise at all (Forster 2014).

Legitimacy (and social power)

Legitimate power is a type of power that depends upon an established and shared set of norms and values and upon people being in agreement about the rules that apply to the group. This type of power is most apparent in those institutions and roles in society that are legitimized by law and which operate through a power that lies outside themselves – written down and consolidated by politicians, police, and courts of law. For instance, legislation on parental rights and responsibilities regarding the child's upbringing and education, which is part of UN's Convention of the Rights of the Child, is an example of this type of power. In some cultures, parental legitimacy is further consolidated through myth and language. For example, respecting your mother "because she gave birth to you" might be a strong social norm. Legitimate power, which is consolidated by law, is often easier for parents to enforce because it is beyond doubt: "That's just the way it is. That's the law." Most parents know that it is easier to convince their teenager to wear a seatbelt in the car than to wear a bike helmet.

Legitimate power is not only about legal rules. There are also unspoken rules, norms, and values that a culture or a group agree on. You can be up against strong powers and risk facing social expulsion by violating these rules. An example of an unspoken rule is that you usually only receive Christmas presents from those people to whom you give presents in return. An aunt who happily receives presents from others, year after year, yet never gives any presents herself runs the risk not only of people stopping giving her presents, but of being socially excluded (perhaps not even invited for Christmas). Another example of an unspoken rule that is, however, strictly adhered to is queuing. A person who pushes in front of others in a long queue at the supermarket will be met with protest from the rest of the group (the other people in the queue), as they will react to the violation of an unspoken rule.

The following is an example of how easy it is to uphold rules that are based on laws, even though your role is not ascribed legitimate power:

Eleven-year-old Laura has posted some images of her friend wearing a bikini on her Instagram page. Her stepmother tries to talk to her about removing the images from her account. Laura responds: "That is not up to you. You are not my mom." The stepmother waits a while, then says: "Actually, it is illegal to post nude pictures of others." "Who asked for your opinion," is Laura's response, before she slams the door to her room. Five minutes later, however, the pictures are gone.

Laura's stepmother struggles with a lack of legitimate power as parent, since she is only Laura's stepmother (see the model "the Lighthouse – giving and receiving authority," p. 53). However, the fact that it is illegal to post images of scantily clad people on Instagram without their consent is a type of legitimate power that Laura can understand.

You can also use the group to legitimize your power. Inspired by Gandhi, Haim Omer (2004), an Israeli psychologist, has researched how sociality can be used as a powerful force, since being part of a group entails the risk of being excluded. According to Omer, publicly verbalizing behaviour that you disapprove of can have a positive impact on children's behaviour: "We won't have dessert until Peter sits in his chair." "I'm sorry, mom, but I have to interrupt this conversation, because Marie just gave me a fuck-off sign." It's important when you use this form of power to realize that it can be interpreted as punishment and have the same consequences. Therefore, it should only be used so often.

Knowledge – being the smarter one

People often say that knowledge is power, and it is true that knowledge plays an important role in the relationship between parent and child. Parents know more about the world than the child does. On the other hand, the child is predisposed for and interested in learning to understand the world they are becoming a part of.

> A mother tries to explain to her daughter about cookies on the Internet, as they are buying tickets for a holiday at a website that appears to be using cookies. Her daughter listens with interest, saying: "I thought those questions that pop up and ask me if I accept cookies were ads for a company selling baked goods, and that if you said yes you might win some."

By explaining to her daughter about cookies, the mother broadens her daughter's knowledge about the world, which will now make more sense to her.

Passing on knowledge allows you to guide your child in how they should understand and interpret their experiences with the world. Knowledge, then, gives parents the power to define the world for their children. It is up to them to determine whether their 1-year-old is behaving badly or curiously exploring the world when he is playing with his food.

Parents also define their child's social world: Do we believe in God? Which politicians are trustworthy, and which are not? Should you eat organic or not? However, the power of being the smarter one who defines the world is not something parents hold indefinitely. Although knowledge is a powerful resource, it will weaken as the child grows older. Maybe your child will not quickly overtake you as the smarter one, but they will know more about certain things than their parents do. Just consider technological inventions and current cultural topics. More often than not, parents have a hard time keeping pace with their children in these areas.

A father is considered almost omniscient by his family. When his two sons or his wife discuss something, it always ends in: "Just ask dad!" As the children grow older, the eldest quickly comes to know more about computers and apps than his father. The father also perceives that his son does not ask for his help with his homework anymore, and it wrings his heart when his sons says: "You don't know anything about that–I'll figure it out myself." The biggest crisis, however, arises when his son, now 11 years old, refuses to listen to his father's knowledge about football anymore and becomes a Chelsea fan even though his father always taught him to support Tottenham.

In this example, the father ceases to be the smarter one who has the power to define the world for his son – for example in terms of which football team is the best one. At this point, if the father does not seize the next – and last – form of power, the boy's teenage years might be difficult.

Epistemic trust – RAM

Originally, this form of power was called referent power (French & Raven 1959), and it has a lot in common with the important concept of epistemic trust, which belongs in mentalization theory.

Epistemic trust has to do with the fact that the child must have trust in another person to teach it something personally relevant, generalizable and that the child experiences as valuable (Fonagy & Allison 2014; Bateman & Fonagy 2012). As we have already pointed out, this is the most important phenomenon for determining whether a child is ready to learn. Children are by nature vigilant. By vigilance we do not mean the absence of trust – but rather the opposite of blind trust (Sperber et al. 2010). This creates a learning filter; when vigilance is activated, the door to learning is closed. The problem is not having a natural vigilance. The problem is when vigilance is the most prominent.

So how do you activate a child's epistemic trust? How do you replace the child's natural hypervigilance with epistemic trust? Simply by being someone the child wants to learn from and whose mind seems more mature. That is done by using signals or cues called ostensive cues. Cues from the caregiver include eye contact, a motherese tone of voice and being open to the responsiveness of the child (ibid.).

So activating epistemic trust involves simply being someone the child wants to learn from, whose mind seems more mature, who takes responsibility for the child's development and learning, and who seems interested in the child as an agent – in short, someone who is regulated and accountable and someone who understands themselves as well as the child – that is, someone who is more mentalizing. Parents who are regulated, accountable, and mentalizing (RAM) inspire epistemic trust in their children.

Regulated

The child trusts a parent who is regulated and therefore able to act as a role model for the child and who can teach them how to regulate their emotions, all the while maintaining their own mentalization. This means that the parent has to lead the way in terms of robust mentalization rather than passing on mentalization failure. Such situations, where the parent acts as a role model and is able to stay mentalizing, forms the basis of the child's epistemic trust (Fonagy et al. 2014). Caregivers who are able to self-regulate will be regarded as natural authorities, and parents who are able to regulate their emotions will automatically be seen as having a more mature mind. A child who experiences a parent who is able to self-regulate lets go of their hypervigilance.

> A father to a newborn hears his eldest daughter, who is briefly watching the new baby while her mother is at the doctor, calling desperately from the living room. She is bent over her baby brother, who has blue lips and is convulsing. The father can see the fear in the boy's eyes, and his daughter yells at him in despair. The father feels his own powerlessness but manages to regulate himself. He asks his daughter to take the baby's clothes off since the convulsions are probably caused by a sudden fever. He stays calm and calls 911 while watching his daughter do as told and sees the baby's convulsions starting to subside. Because of her father staying regulated, the daughter was actually able to save her little brother.

This might be a somewhat dramatic example, but there are many situations in the everyday life of a family that require parents to regulate themselves and show that they have the more mature mind.

When the parent wants the child to pay attention to something, the parent who is able to regulate himself can use a special regulated tone of voice (motherese) which seem specially attuned to the child. And the parent can regulate the dialogue so there is room for turn taking. The ability to regulate oneself and on top of a feeling or situation is also part of the normal, developmental interaction where the child becomes their own person and which teaches the child to regulate their emotions.

Accountable

Children trust parents who signals accountability and are able to create a safe environment that encourages the child to embrace learning. Parent who are able to set boundaries create a structure which is initially found in the world outside the child but which is later internalized by the child. In addition, accountable parents make decisions that are meaningful and are able to exercise leadership. Humans have been living in hierarchies for a long time and will happily conform to a hierarchy in which power is administered justly and meaningfully and which ensures a minimum of conflict. A hierarchy can create safety and meaning, for example a family where the parents lead the way in creating a safe group that moves in a meaningful and responsible direction. Such parents make sure their children go to school and brush their teeth; they create a safe and positive environment, etc.

In order to be accountable in regard to small children, parents must work together to set boundaries and create a safe environment for the child: how we eat, when we go to bed, when we get up in the morning, who takes care of which household chores etc. Teenagers are particularly challenging because parents have to be accountable and able to let go at the same time.

A mother has just tucked her exhausted daughter in after a children's Christmas party. The mother has been acting responsibly all day: She made sure her daughter ate real food before she had candy. She resolved a dispute between her daughter and a friend who wanted to have a sleepover but who were clearly too tired. She made sure that her daughter brushed her teeth, read her a bedtime story, and answered all her questions. Finally, she has some peace and drops into the couch with a box of candy bars that Santa had given her daughter at the Christmas party. Her daughter unexpectedly enters the living room, saying: "Mommy, what are you eating?" The mother automatically answers "Nothing," but then realizes that she is supposed to be an accountable and honest role model for her daughter. "I'm sorry," she says. "I am eating one of your candy bars." The girl protests. The mother understands her but sticks to the rule that candy is not allowed after toothbrushing, and she promises to buy her new candy bars tomorrow.

Despite her somewhat irresponsible handling of candy, the mother succeeds in getting back on track with being an accountable role model for appropriate behaviour as well as conflict resolution.

Mentalizing

Children have more trust in parents who are able to mentalize, understand their own and others' minds, and re-establish and maintain a mentalizing approach. When children feel that their personal narrative is understood by the parents, they let go of their hypervigilance and learn to mentalize themselves. This provides a basis for creating an environment that encourages children to listen and consider the knowledge and perspectives of others.

Two-year-old Sarah is not very kind to her new baby sister. Sarah's mother understands that Sarah misses the time where she had her parents to herself and that becoming a big sister is a major change for her. Since Sarah is yet not old enough to understand her sister's needs, her mother tells her: "I know that it is annoying to have a baby sister – let's go take a look at your new scooter, just you and me; I haven't had time to see how good you are at riding it."

According to the theory, mentalization is generally a process that works inside-out. The parents are the ones who mentalize with the child, and through this interaction the child learns to mentalize as well. Much of this is learned through the early interaction between mother and child, but if this is not the case, the good thing about the mentalization theory is that it holds the possibility for lifelong development. However, this presupposes that you want to be a parent who understands how the human mind works – and that, as a child, you follow your parents' example.

RAM placed in a lighthouse

In a computer, RAM is a part of the memory which is present and instantly accessible. Likewise, in a conflict, parents must have easy access to the mentalizing part of their mind. It could be during a conflict with their child, where the parent is close to experiencing mentalization failure themselves – for instance, when having to pick up your drunk teenager from a "movie night" with their friends, going shopping with your 2-year-old who demands ice cream, or standing in a dark hallway in the middle of the night with a child who will not go to sleep. The following example illustrates how the three concepts of RAM can be the only necessary forms of power.

Twelve-year-old Mia has always been a happy, outgoing girl with lots of friends. One day, however, this changes overnight. It happens at a party where Mia's classmates have arranged carpooling, but it turns out that there is room for everyone but Mia. Mia asks her parents to drive her to the party, where she hangs out with some girls from another class. They are loyal to Mia and tell her classmates that it is not okay for them to exclude Mia. This results in tears, and afterwards Mia's classmates are very cold towards her. From having friends over every day, now Mia never has plans with anyone. Mia isolates herself, stays in her room, and is short-tempered and aggressive at home. Mia's mother feels herself becoming irritated with her. One day, Mia yells at her mother, and the mother wants to yell back: "Maybe there's a reason why your friends won't hang out with you anymore!" But she stops herself, reminds herself that she is the grown-up who needs to stay regulated She also needs to be account-able and help Mia resolve the dispute with her classmates, and finally, she needs to stay mentalizing. She needs to mentalize Mia but also the class-mates who have excluded her. Their mothers are generally nice, so Mia's mother tries to be a lighthouse: the one who invites the other mothers over to talk about the issue, and this meeting ends up affecting the girl group positively.

Regulated Accountable Mentalizing

Figure 0.5 RAM

In the remainder of this book, *the lighthouse* with RAM will be used to illustrate the most effective form of power available to parents in terms of asserting and maintaining authority over their child. In Figure 0.5, RAM is placed at the top of a lighthouse. The lighthouse is a metaphor for parents who stay — regulated, accountable, and mentalizing — on a solid foundation that cannot be toppled or washed over. They are able to look at the bigger picture and to enlighten themselves as well as their child when the latter faces rough, turbulent waters. They are also able to turn on the light in their children so that they are able to shine a light on themselves and, later, on others (Byrne 2016).

Chapter 1

Mentalizing – basic concepts

We now turn to the basic concepts in mentalization regarding parenting. In the following, we examine the concepts of mentalization, mentalization failure, and the circle of mentalization failure. The counterpart to mentalization failure – the open-mind approach – will also be described, followed by a model illustrating power and authority.

We also examine a few concepts relating to mentalization and the brain. The brain is a popular organ these days – and rightly so, since we have learned a lot about the workings of the brain within the past few decades. However, it is important to remember that there is still a lot we do not know about the brain. For example, the images that are recorded when a person is experiencing a certain state are fairly unstable, as they will change if the person is holding someone's hand, for instance (Hari et al. 2015). So although knowledge of the brain will help us to better understand our children and their interaction, it is important to only use this knowledge to support mentalization and understanding of your child and to not reduce your child or yourself to simply a brain.

Mentalization

Mentalization is about perceiving and understanding your own and others' behaviour based on mental states, that is emotions, needs, goals, reasons, and thoughts. The mentalization approach is particularly well suited for working with children and adolescents because it offers a complete theory on how to best support child development. Mentalization is a capacity that the child will acquire if adults mentalize in their interaction with the child.

On the face of it, mentalization might appear simple and self-evident. But when you start working with the concept it often turns out to be more complicated than first anticipated. Figure 1.1 might help you understand the meaning of mentalization.

Suggestions and strategies

Mentalize yourself first – and then your child. When you mentalize, you are able to regulate your own emotions. It is important to remember that the model is a simplified representation of reality, since mentalization is notions about your own and others' mental states. This means that the mental states of everyone involved in a situation are important – that includes both the parent and the child who are interacting but also the sister who is listening and the other parent, who might be the subject of the conversation.

Example

A mother reads in a magazine that too many people place their couch against the wall. She experiments by moving the couch to the middle of the room, and it works brilliantly. The father and older sister agree, but the family's youngest, 12-year-old Mike, does not. While the other three are out shopping, Mike drags the sofa back to its place against the wall with difficulty. When the rest of the family returns, his mother becomes angry, telling Mike that it is not up to him to decide how their home should be furnished. She only just manages to stay mentalizing. First, herself – she feels angry, but also powerless (feelings). Her thoughts revolve around the idea that "no one respects me." She does not feel that her good idea is recognized (need), namely, to have a nice home (goal). When she was a child, she was living with old, used furniture that she had no part in choosing, and she was always embarrassed about her room (reasons). In regard to her son, she knows that he is scared and sad (feelings). Mike needs things to be clear and foreseeable, and he does not like change (need). Mike has recently experienced some challenges at school, and he attempts to make order out of chaos and create a refuge for himself (goal and reasons).

The fact that the mother is able to go through this small process enables her to approach Mike with better regulated emotions and talk to him about the reason why the couch should be placed in the middle of the room. Mike then asks if it can be moved to its old spot on his birthday, which is in a month. "On your birthday, you get to decide where the couch should be placed," she answers.

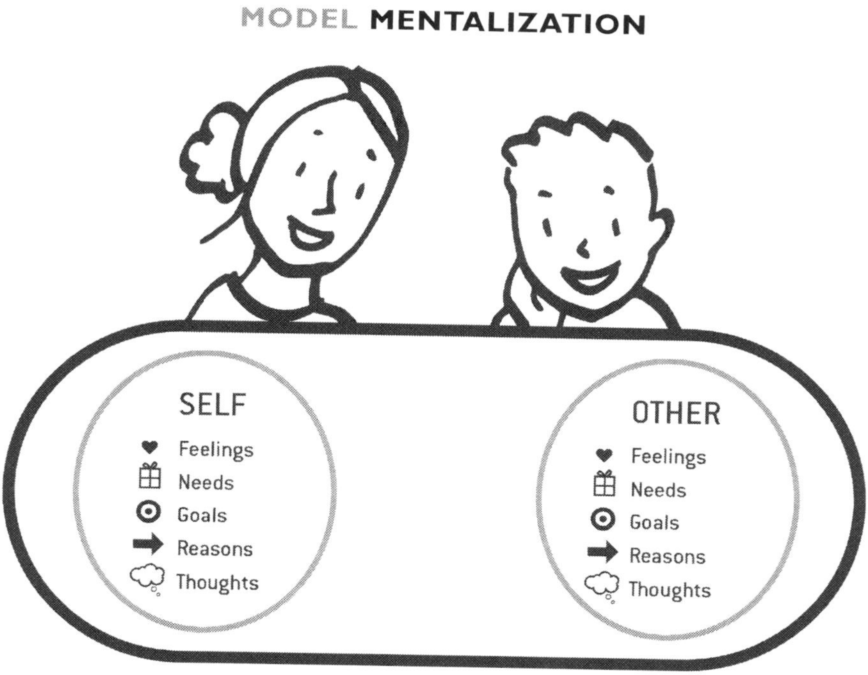

MODEL **MENTALIZATION**

Figure 1.1

How do you do it?

- Other ways to talk about mentalization are: "paying attention to your own and others' mental states," "understanding misunderstandings," "looking at yourself from the outside and the other person from the inside," and "looking beyond behaviour."
- When you experience intense emotions and thoughts, attempt to actively consider what is going on in your own mind as well as what is going on in your child's mind.
- Mentalization is like learning to ride a bike. At the beginning you have to think a lot about what you are doing, but as you progress, the process becomes automatic. But take care that you don't rely too much on your automatic mentalizing, as it sometimes can trick you. You just have to stay actively thinking about mental states.
- By staying curious about the mental processes that lie behind behaviour, you exercise your "mentalization-muscle."
- You can never know exactly what is going on in another person's mind, so your task is to try to guess and be open to the fact that many things can be happening simultaneously in other people's minds.
- Mentalization is an important part of having a positive, united sense of self, as well as of our emotions and relations to others.
- Mentalization is a particularly useful tool to be used in conflicts.

Mentalization failure

Mentalization failure happens when you lose your focus on your own and others' mental states. This means losing touch with your own emotions, needs, goals, reasons, and thoughts – as well as the other person's. The capacity for mentalization can fail, for instance, under intense emotional agitation or when you feel threatened (Bateman & Fonagy 2007). Children typically experience many mentalization failures because they have not yet developed the capacity for mentalization. As an adult, you should attempt to not let yourself be affected by this and instead be a role model for mentalization, since the child cannot do it on its own.

Everyone experiences mentalization failure – and usually many, both big and small, every day. Some people react explosively and heatedly to mentalization failure. Others simply shut down, become silent, and appear calm, yet they are not in touch with their own or others' mental state.

Suggestions and strategies

Mentalization failures should be regarded as interesting and challenging opportunities for exercising your own as well as your child's capacity for mentalization. Figure 1.2 can be used for talking to other adults and older children about what happens just before a mentalization failure, while you were headed down a black hole and were unable to understand either yourself or the other person.

When you are on your way back to being able to mentalize, the ability is fragile and breaks down more easily, especially if others challenge you. When your capacity for mentalization is restored, you are able to look at the situation in quite a different light.

Example

A father has just woken up his two daughters, who are 9 and 14 years old. He chats with them from the bathroom, and suddenly remembers that his eldest daughter, Leah, needs her clean gym shorts for school today. He enters her room, saying: "Look what I've washed for you, so they're ready for today." Just when he is half a step inside Leah's room, she slams the door in his face and yells: "GET OUT, you idiot!"

The father gets angry; the door almost hit him right in his face. He kicks the closed door before stomping into his other daughter's room. She is still lying in her bed, looking at her phone. He yells at her: "Get up, right now! What the hell do you think you are doing? You aren't allowed to look at that shit. GET UP, now!" He leaves, walks past Leah's door again, and kicks it again while yelling: "I'm leaving – I can't take this madhouse any longer, and there is no birthday party this weekend, do you understand?"

MODEL MENTALIZATION FAILURE

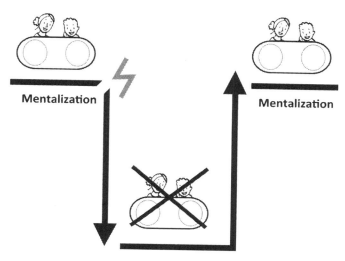

Figure 1.2

How do you do it?

- The more you are aware of the risk of mentalization failure, the better you are able to understand yourself and your triggers (that is, situations that remind you of other, similar negative situations and which activate intense emotions such as anxiety, anger, or stress).
- The more you are aware of the risk of mentalization failure, the better you are able to understand your child and its own triggers.
- When your child experiences a mentalization failure, the most important thing to do is to remain calm and mentalizing yourself.
- When you are unable to mentalize yourself, you cannot help others mentalize.

The vicious circle

Mentalization failure can be described as a vicious circle which begins when you experience intense emotions. Intense emotions lead to poor mentalization, which means that it becomes difficult to understand others and you start making negative assumptions about the other person's thoughts and feelings. You might act based on these assumptions, and this affects the way that others think and feel. As a consequence, they might act in a way that further intensifies your own emotions. In this way, the vicious circle can continue and spread to others.

Suggestions and strategies

It is a good idea to be aware, firstly, of the risk of starting up or becoming a part of this very common vicious circle, and secondly, that you are able to change such negative spirals yourself by maintaining your capacity for mentalization.

Example

After a long week, 6-year-old Lisa is out shopping with her father on a Friday night. Lisa is very frustrated and says: "I want my candy." Her father gets angry, saying: "We have talked about this so many times. You are allowed have some candy on Friday night, but this is way too much." He snatches the bag of candy from her hand (intense emotions and poor mentalization) and returns many of the contents to their shelves. Lisa says: "Dad, you've taken out my favourite candy!" The father replies: "Just stop it, Lisa" (poor ability to understand others' emotions). Lisa says: "Dad, please; it's the ones shaped like clowns that I like so much." Her father feels provoked, thinking: "She has no sympathy for the fact that I am tired, and she tries to make a fool of me here where people I know can see how she humiliates me" (making assumptions about what other people think and feel). Lisa says again: "I promise I won't spend too much, but can I please just have the candy that is shaped like clowns?" The father hisses at her: "You are so selfish, trying to ruin everything for me. Forget about it" (starts to react based on these assumptions). Lisa starts to cry, throws all of the candy on the floor, and will not listen to her father at all (behaviour affects the child's thoughts and emotions).

MODEL **VICIOUS CIRCLE**

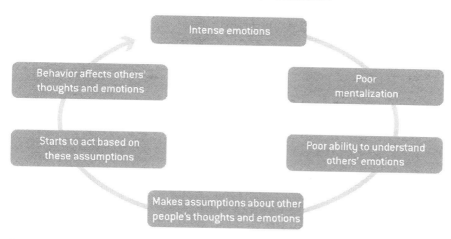

Figure 1.3

How do you do it?

- Pay attention to the way in which intense emotions lead to mentalization failure – break the vicious circle.
- The first person to become aware of a mentalization failure must bring mentalization back into the interaction.
- It is always the adults' responsibility to support the recovery of mentalization when mentalization failure happens between children and adults.

An open mind

In order to support your child's development, you must continually try to imagine what is going on in the child's mind. It is impossible to know, and part of being a mentalizing parent is to attempt to look at things from your own perspective as well as your child's. As a parent, it is easy to make the mistake of focusing on the child's behaviour instead of what lies behind the child's behaviour. If you attempt to keep an open mind, it is possible to turn down the intensity of your own emotions, which enables you to understand what it is important for your child to learn. One way to help yourself keep an open mind is to remember the "open-mind approach," which is based on openness, patience, empathy, balance, empathy, and curiosity (Hagelquist 2012, 2015).

Suggestions and strategies

In order to help the child learn something new and understand themselves and others, you must focus on what goes on in your own mind as well as in the child's mind.

Example

Three-year-old Luke is digging a hole in the family's lawn. When his father sees it, he becomes really angry because the entire family had spent last weekend filling it up with earth, levelling, and finally sowing grass. The father has already explained to Luke that you are only allowed to dig in the sandbox. The father remembers to keep an open mind and lets go of his first notion that Luke is only doing it to annoy him. He considers the fact that he has his own needs when it comes to the lawn and that Luke's needs are different. He tries to show empathy towards Luke's perspective and reaches the conclusion that Luke must be proud of the nice hole he has been digging. The father tries to be curious about the reason why Luke has been digging in the lawn and remembers that Luke was watching admiringly as the rest of the family were working in the garden last weekend. He thinks that it will probably be some time before a 3-year-old is able to understand that it is okay to dig in the lawn in some situations, but not in others.

MODEL OF AN OPEN MIND

Openness

The parent meets the child with openness when they forget their first assumptions about what is going on and try to keep all options open. Here, you keep your mind open and avoid inflexible hypotheses.

Balance

Balancing oneself is hard, but it is about making room for your own perspective as well as being aware of the child's. Sometimes you might even have to consider younger siblings' minds or your partner's mind on top of it all.

Empathy

Empathy is essential to mentalization and has to do with putting yourself in the child's place, so in a way the balance is tilted towards the child, but the more empathy you show towards your child, the more secure the child will feel.

Curiosity

When you feel angry or frustrated it can be hard to be curious. But asking why is the best way to understand what lies behind someone's behavior. Children of varying ages have different challenges when it comes to explaining themselves. Even teenagers might not be able to explain their behavior or want to keep it to themselves what is happening on the inside. In these cases, it is a question of being curious, guessing, and having plenty of possible imaginative explanations.

Patience

Raising children is a long process. It takes patience, both in each individual conflict and in the long run. Sometimes you lose your sense of direction and worry that the child's development is moving in the wrong direction. There is no straight line when it comes to development but rather fluctuations, periods without development, or breaks in the developmental curve. First and foremost, however, it is individual. Nature has challenged us that way, but fortunately it means that you learn a lot about yourself and your child along the way.

Figure 1.4

How do you do it?

In order to keep an open mind, ask yourself the following questions:

- Do I stay open and flexible when it comes to understanding my child's behaviour? _____
- Am I balanced in terms of looking at the situation from different perspectives? _____
- Am I able to feel empathy towards my child? _____
- Am I genuinely curious about what lies behind the behaviour? _____
- Do I have the time and patience to deal with this properly? _____

Power and authority

Children are born with competencies and abilities, but they are basically part of an asymmetrical relation in which the parents know more about the world than their child, at least when their child is young. The knowledge and support of their parents is an important part of children's development. When parents feel that their child starts breaking this asymmetry and acts as if he is the one in charge, as a parent, you often feel powerless and start looking for ways to regain authority. This makes the concept of power interesting in relation to parenting.

Power can be divided into five subtypes: punishment, reward, legitimate power, knowledge, and epistemic trust (French & Raven 1959). As a parent, you might need all of these different types of power, but epistemic trust is the most important one for modern parenting. It consists of being someone you want to learn from, that is, someone who is: Regulated, Accountable, and Mentalizing. Epistemic trust is also about being a role model in terms of exercising power.

Suggestions and strategies

When the child acts inappropriately and the parent experiences intense emotions and mentalization failure, punishment is often the form of power that they resort to. In the moment, it might seem like the right choice. In fact, humans are predisposed to deriving brief satisfaction from punishing inappropriate behaviour, but in the long term the child learns nothing from this, and parents run the risk of the child losing their trust in them as a teacher and role model.

Example

Fourteen-year-old Louisa tells her mother that she is going to a party at a friend's house the following Friday and that she intends to sleep over. Her mother says: "But we agreed that you are only allowed to have sleepovers with friends if I have spoken to their parents." Louisa replies: "You can't tell me what to do. I'll just go without telling you where the party is." The mother wants to threaten Louisa that she will take away her pocket money or ground her (punishment) but instead attempts to remain a mother who is regulated, accountable, and mentalizing, and says: "You are not allowed to do that, but I would be happy to drive you and your friends to the party" (reward). "Don't tell me what to do. I'll do what I please," Louisa says. The mother, however, knows that she is the one in charge (legitimate power). "What are you going to do about it," Louisa says. "I want us to come to an agreement, but if we can't, I could always just come to the party, sit at the bar, and hang out a little," the mother says, knowing that this would be the ultimate punishment for a teenager.

MODEL **POWER**

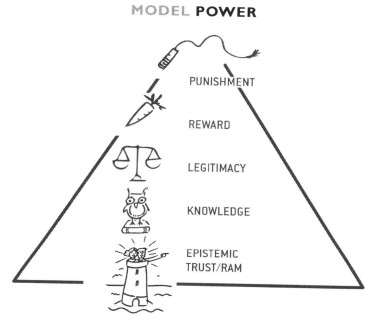

PUNISHMENT

REWARD

LEGITIMACY

KNOWLEDGE

EPISTEMIC TRUST/RAM

Figure 1.5

How do you do it?

Mainly use the forms of power from the bottom of the power pyramid.

Punishment

Can be threats, natural consequences, or taking away privileges.

- Punishment removes trust, and we need to trust someone in order to learn from them.
- Children do not really learn from negative consequences. Think about children who fall when they are learning to walk – fortunately, they just keep on trying.
- When using punishment, it is important to reflect: "Is this the way I want to teach my child to handle conflicts?"

Reward

Receiving something of value or a social activity as reward/praise.

- When the reward is removed, the rewarded behaviour might also disappear.
- An expensive and time-consuming solution.
- Rewards can lead to rivalry between children about what is and is not fair.

Legitimate power

We are social creatures and have established shared norms and values. Our desire to be part of the group means that we have a natural tendency to subject ourselves to shared social norms.

- It is easy to assert that you cannot do something that is illegal. But it is somewhat limiting as the only form of power.

Knowledge

Children *want* to learn, and they seek out and happily subject themselves to someone who is more knowledgeable.

- Knowing more than your child and wanting to share this knowledge is an important form of power.
- At some point, your knowledge will run out and your child will know more than you.

Epistemic trust (RAM)

A child wants to follow a parent who is regulated, accountable, and mentalizing, because they sense that there is a possibility for development. With such a parent, the child can feel secure and trust in the parent to led them in the right direction.

Mirror neurons

In 1996, a group of Italian neurologists discovered something that is known today as mirror neurons (Gallese et al. 1996). They discovered the phenomenon during a scientific experiment in which they were investigating the activity in the brain of a monkey while it was making deliberate movements with its hand and mouth. By coincidence, the scientists discovered that there was also activity in the monkey's brain when it observed them grasping and moving the piece of fruit they were going to give the monkey. The neurons in the monkey's brain were mirroring the scientists' behaviour.

This led to the knowledge that brain cells "mirror" others' meaningful behaviour. Since then, further research into this area has established that when we perceive an intention, an emotion, or a train of thought in another person, these experiences are mirrored in our own mind, because it activates mirror neurons. Hence, the system of mirror neurons forms the basis of phenomena such as imitation, mirroring, resonance, empathy, sympathy, identification, internalization, intersubjectivity, and mentalization, but also the phenomena of emotional contagion and emotional fusion (Koefoed & Visholm 2011).

There are many examples of phenomena that can be described based on the theory of mirror neurons. It is possible to observe the effect of mirror neurons, for instance, if a parent is able to create a synchronized consensus in the family through facial expressions, which creates a positive sense of togetherness and "we"-feeling. Mirror neurons help us interpret other people's intentions, but they seldom leave a lasting, strong impression. The feeling only sticks when memories, language, and emotions are tied together. If you, as parents, are affected by difficult or intense emotions, it can be helpful for the child to learn to be able to talk about the signals that it can feel emanating from its parents, so that emotions are not allowed to flow uncontrollably and without meaning.

Suggestions and strategies

Emotions such as anxiety, shame, and stress are highly contagious. Be aware of these emotions in yourself, and how you regulate them, before they spread to your family.

Example

Two 9-year-old girls start laughing during a maths lesson. Every time they look at each other, they start over. The maths teacher gets angry, but when he sees that all the girls have started laughing, he involuntarily starts laughing too. Mirror neurons are at work.

MODEL **MIRROR NEURONS**

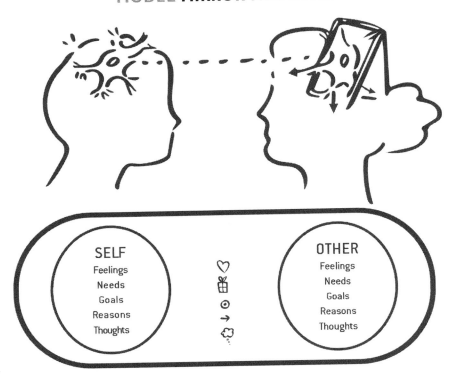

Figure 1.6

How do you do it?

- Be careful about demanding eye contact when dealing with feelings such as anger, anxiety, sadness, or disgust. Eye contact leads to emotional contagion and can escalate the conflict.
- Sit next to the child or below the child's eye level when you are having difficult conversations.
- Distract and regulate the child when he or she is experiencing intense feelings, so that the child's emotions do not spread to you.
- Be aware that when you are experiencing intense feelings, your state of mind is highly contagious. Regulate yourself.
- Make active use of mirror neurons when you want your child to do something. For example, if you want your child to clean their room, then start cleaning the house yourself and count on activating the mirror neurons in your child that have to do with grasping things and putting it away.

The triune brain

The triune brain is a way of describing the human brain in terms of its evolution. The lower part of the brain originates in the primitive reptilian brain which deals with autonomic processes. When this part of the brain is active, the possible lines of action are fight, flight, or freeze. Later, we developed into mammals, and this is where the next part of the brain originates. This part, known as the limbic system or the mammalian brain, deals with emotions and attachment. The highest part of the brain is the neocortex, or what we may call "the thinking brain." In evolutionary terms, this part of the brain is the newest. The thinking brain contains language, reason, and planning skills. Essential brain functions related to mentalization is also found in this part of the brain.

The higher functions of the brain are only able to operate on the basis of the lower functions, whereas the lower functions are independent of the higher functions. That is, when humans are overcome by their emotions, they use the more primitive parts of the brain, and in such situations there is only limited access to the more rational parts of the brain that deal with mentalization, decision making, and the ability to take a comprehensive view of the situation. When you are trying to explain something to a child who is very upset, it will be like talking to a brick wall. The child must be calmed down before it is possible to get through to the thinking brain. Part of supporting children's development is to ensure that all three parts of the brain learn to work together (Siegel & Bryson 2014).

Suggestions and strategies

Figure 1.7 is a way of illustrating the complex processes that are activated when one experiences intense emotions. But it is just a model – in reality, these are highly complex brain functions, and as we have already pointed out, the brain works as a coherent, integral unit.

Example

A mother picks up her two children from their gymnastics practice after a long day. As she parks the car in the driveway, her daughter says: "I forgot my school bag!" The mother states: "Well, you can't do without it," and starts backing the car. Meanwhile, the family's cat has settled down under the car, and they run over the cat. Its neck is broken, but it is still moving.

The mother regresses to her reptilian brain and stares at the cat (freeze). She then has an impulse to run it over again "so that it won't suffer" (fight). Her daughter starts to cry, and she wants to drive away (flight). She looks at her children and starts to mentalize. This brings her back up to her thinking brain, and she says: "Don't worry, I'll handle it." She gets out of the car and gently strokes the cat, which dies peacefully. Afterwards, she comforts the children, and they organize a funeral for the cat.

MODEL THE BRAIN AND MENTALIZATION FAILURE

Figure 1.7

How do you do it?

Be aware that:

- When your child is in the reptilian brain, its focus is survival, and it will react with either fight, flight, or freeze – the task is to make the child feel safe and secure – at this stage, learning is impossible.
- When your child is in the mammalian brain, its emotions are at work, generally being: anger, anxiety, and sadness.
- When your child is in the thinking part of the brain, the conditions for learning are at their optimum and the child is able to listen to and

understand what you are saying. At this stage, it is important that you are aware of what exactly it is that you want your child to learn.

- When you are in your reptilian brain, you are unable to help your child but have to regulate yourself so that you can get back to the thinking part of your brain.
- Help your child improve their ability to integrate reptilian brain, mammalian brain, and thinking brain.
- If you have older children, you can show them the model of the triune brain and fight, flight, and freeze.

Chapter 2

The nautical universe

We have decided to use a nautical universe to illustrate the basic elements of a parenting style that stimulates and supports child development in the best possible way. The seafaring universe is well suited for illustrating mentalizing parenting, because it contains the ocean, ships, gangways, storms, and the marine environment, which are already used elsewhere in mentalization theory to describe human development, developmental journeys, and existential challenges (Byrne 2016; Hagelquist 2012). The nautical universe offers an abundance of imagery, including metaphors and phrases such as being the captain of one's own ship or being in deep waters. More specifically, we use the ship as a metaphor for the child – a ship (the child) that needs to be prepared for its journey and loaded with a cargo of knowledge about itself and the surrounding world, ready to leave its safe harbour and experience the world on its own. The ocean is a force of nature that the child must learn to master before he can finally set sail with a cargo full of abilities.

The ocean also functions well as a symbol of the many experiences and challenges of parenthood, since the universe of natural forces makes it possible for us to illustrate parenthood as a state where we are able to enjoy days of calm water but where we also experience days of high sea, with storm, waves, and intense, uncontrollable natural forces.

On the following pages, child development and your role as a parent will be described as a seafaring adventure featuring ships, lighthouses, compasses, waves, and storms – safe voyage!

The child – the ship

When a child is born, it is helpless and depends on others to satisfy its basic needs in order to survive. However, it is also born with great potentials – a range of inherent characteristics and latent abilities, such as the ability to enter into social relationships. By interacting with its caregivers and with the environment, the child will develop these potentials throughout its childhood.

It is also possible to talk about these things from a more biological point of view, since recent findings in epigenetics describe how the environment affects certain parts of the child's DNA and thereby determines which "parts" of the child are activated and which remain dormant in certain situations.

In the nautical universe, the child is viewed as a ship loaded with developmental opportunities. In the same way that there are thousands of children in the world who are all different and unique in their own way, there are also thousands of different ships; large and small, fast and slow: pirate ships and sailing vessels, speedboats and dinghies, ferries, cargo vessels, and toy ships. For parents, the task is to see their child as a unique and beautiful ship and to support it and make it ready to set sail for the seven seas – including an occasional trip home.

The child is predisposed for developing a wide range of abilities. He or she might have a smaller or a larger inborn potential for developing these abilities, but *how* they are developed depends on the way in which the child is treated from infancy throughout childhood. There will be stages where it is easier for the child to develop certain abilities. For instance, it is much easier for toddlers to learn a language than for older children or adults, because the child is naturally preoccupied with sounds and language at this stage of its development. If the child is not presented with the opportunity to learn a language at this critical stage, its potential for language will not be developed, and it will be harder for the child to learn a language at a later stage.

Suggestions and strategies

Consider the child's full potential – look at your child as a small ship that has just been built, but also consider what they might become. Support them, and keep in mind a positive image of your child's potential.

Example

A mother is breastfeeding her daughter Molly, who is 8 weeks old. While looking at her lovingly, she says: "I can't believe that people ever believed that children are the same when they are born. Molly is such a different person than her sister. She is so curious and intense in our interaction. Her sister Clara was much more subtly reserved, but also self-contained, and you really had to work to get her attention. Even though she is 7 years old now, she is still like that."

MODEL **THE CHILD – THE SHIP**

Figure 2.1

How do you do it?

- See your child as a unique human being.
- Support your child's development, so they can reach their potential.
- Throughout your child's development, it can be frustrating that your "little ship" is not the way you might want it to be. Keep in mind that you need to see the child's potential and resources in order for the child to develop them.
- It can be a good idea to imagine the kind of ship you want your child to become, but it is easy to make the mistake of projecting your own ship onto the child. Remember that your child is their own unique little ship.
- Find a balance between guiding the ship and working towards the ship being able to sail on its own.

A safe harbour

When a child is securely attached to another person, this person acts as a safe base from which the child can explore its environment. The child has a safe harbour that it can return to for care and understanding. This teaches the child that it is worthwhile to seek contact and reach out to others – it has a positive effect. Furthermore, this sense of safety creates a safe, peaceful environment that allows the child to focus its attention on exploring the surrounding world. The theory about a safe base or harbour has produced some of the most stable psychological research, originating all the way back to Bowlby's attachment theory (1969).

Children must be able to rely on a safe and harmonious relation to their primary caregiver before they dare venture out to explore the world. Part of this sense of security is to have a safe base to venture out from and a safe harbour to return to. So if we use a ship as a symbol of the child, it has to feel secure enough to leave its safe harbour – so safe that it dares to leave its secure base and go to sea, and so safe that it dares go back into the safe harbour. The concept of a "safe harbour" covers both "safe base" and "safe harbour." In the following text we use the term "Safe Harbour" which covers both "Secure base" and "safe harbour."

Suggestions and strategies

It is important to provide the child with a safe harbour in the form of a safe physical home as well as a secure relationship. This attachment relation must be able to contain negative as well as positive aspects.

It is important that the child feels secure with its parents. If they are a source of anxiety, punishment, and failure, you run the risk of depriving the child of the most important element of its possibility for development. If you do not have a safe harbour, you do not have the energy to explore and learn about the world.

Example

Three-year-old Jonathan has just started kindergarten. When his mother arrives to pick him up, he does not want to go into the stroller but wants her to carry him. As she is cooking dinner, he again wants her to pick him up. He hugs her leg and says: "Up, up!" Jonathan no longer wants his father to tuck him in, and he will not go to sleep unless his mother lies next to him until he falls asleep. Usually, this takes up the entire evening. The mother becomes more and more desperate and feels like pushing Jonathan far away. But a friend tells her that the reason why he acts this way is because he needs her to be his safe harbour. "Perhaps you need to really make him your priority and show him that you will always be there. Because of all this change, what with starting kindergarten and everything, he might need to know that you are there for him. Maybe it is worth it to spend time showing him that he can rely on you as his safe harbour."

The mother pays Jonathan more attention, and on the weekend the father takes his son fishing and makes it a priority for them to spend time together, so that the boy really feels that his mother and father are his safe harbours. Their relation quickly changes for the better, and the mother is surprised that she did not realize what was happening on in her own.

MODEL A SAFE HARBOUR

Safe harbour ⸺⸺⸺⸺⸺⸺⸺   Secure base

Figure 2.2

How do you do it?

- Children need a safe harbour from which they can venture out to explore the world.
- Be available, attentive, and helpful.
- A secure attachment is essential for mentalization.
- A safe harbour is the foundation for activating the child's potential for learning and for them to venture out to experience the world on their own.
- When children feel stressed and under pressure, it is even more important for them to feel that they have a safe harbour.
- If the child is going through a hard time, it can be necessary to actively work on making them feel that their parents are their safe harbour. You can help the child feel this way by doing something nice together: going fishing or shopping or taking them to an amusement park or to the library – something that the child enjoys and is interested in and which brings you close to the child, giving it the sense that you are its safe harbour.
- If you are going through a period in your life where you are irritated at or frustrated with your child, it is particularly important to work on doing something to make you the child's safe harbour again.

Attachment styles

Children learn early on what to expect from relationships with others. Having expectations about how people typically react and how you are supposed to react in return makes the world easier to understand. These expectations are called attachment styles, and they are formed through the child's first interaction with their caregivers (Ainsworth & Bell 1970; Bowlby 1969).

There are four different attachment styles. Secure attachment, which is the most advantageous attachment style, ambivalent attachment, avoidant attachment, and disorganized attachment. These patterns of attachment are developed through a complex interaction between biology and early experiences with attachment to one's primary caregiver(s). One must be careful to not categorically determine a person's attachment style because it is possible to have different patterns of attachment to different people, and it is also possible to revise a disadvantageous attachment style. In addition, everyone contains elements of the insecure attachment styles, even those who are basically securely attached.

Figure 2.3 will help you determine the child's preferred style of attachment and what it might need from its caregivers. The child develops secure attachment when adults are regulated, accountable and mentalizing. Accept your child's attachment style, but the model offers a range of suggestions that you might use to try to challenge your child's style of attachment.

Suggestions and strategies

Research has shown that parents only succeed in being available, attentive, and helpful 50 percent of the time (Allen & Fonagy 2006). When the child feels that its parent is unresponsive, the resultant frustration presents the child with an important developmental lesson, because it has to contemplate what is going on in the adult's mind: Why is she unavailable right now? In this way, the child learns how to cope with not being responded to – so do your best to be regulated, accountable and mentalizing but forgive yourself when you are unsuccessful.

Example

Susan runs a family day care where she looks after four 3-year-old children. Each child has a different attachment style.

- Ethan is upset when his mother leaves, but he is easily consoled and is securely attached to Susan. He plays on his own and explores his surroundings, and if he gets upset, he returns to Susan for comfort. When his mother picks him up he is happy to see her (secure).
- Ann is inconsolable when her mother leaves. Afterwards, Ann keeps close to Susan. As a consequence, she does show curiosity towards her

surroundings and explores little. When her mother arrives to pick her up, Ann starts to cry and is difficult to console (ambivalent).

- Connor displays no emotion when his father drops him off at the day care. He explores his environment, but he seldomly seeks comfort. When his mother picks him up, he goes with her, but he does not show any emotion (avoidant).
- Sophie has had a difficult start in life. She has been ill and hospitalized, and she has been placed in isolation without her parents multiple times. In the day care, Sophie takes up a lot of time and space, and it is impossible to predict how she will react. When her parents or the caregivers depart or return, she might react by freezing, raging, or screaming heartrendingly. It is hard for Sophie to be a part of the everyday life at the day care. She reaches for caregivers in an unsystematic manner and might uncritically sit in a stranger's lap (disorganized).

MODEL ATTACHMENT STYLES

Attachment style		*How can I help my child?*
Secure attachment 	The child feels that it has a safe harbour from which it can safely venture out to explore the world. The child can safely return back home. The child experiences its parents as available, attentive, and helpful.	In order to have a securely attached child and to act as your child's safe harbour, you must be available, regulated, accountable and mentalizing towards your child.
Avoidant attachment 	The child feels that it is best if it takes care of itself. It sails out onto the ocean, and when the world feels dangerous, it simply drifts on without return to shore for comfort. On the surface, it might seem as if the child does not care, does not want contact, and does not want to learn anything from others. However, this is usually an indication that the child has hidden away their emotions deep down in the cargo hold, and that it is difficult for him or her to trust that they will receive help to understand and regulate their emotions if they return to the port.	Be available, regulated, accountable and mentalizing -and encourage your avoidant child to return to the port. Show kindness and pay attention to the child when he or she approaches you. Respond to even small signals and show the child that it is worthwhile to hoist its emotions up from the hold. Respect your child's need for a bigger navigation channel and remember that the child needs more praise and support than it seems to signal.

Figure 2.3

Attachment style		How can I help my child?
Ambivalent attachment 	The child feels insecure and is afraid to venture out to sea. Even the smallest challenges will make the child return to the harbour, but it can be hard to comfort and console them. It can be hard for the child to believe in itself and its abilities, and he or she is often more preoccupied with their relation to the adult than with themselves and their own needs.	Be available, regulated, accountable and mentalizing - and encourage the child to go out to sea and explore the world. Show your child that your trust them and believe in them to be able to take care of themselves. Encourage your child to trust themselves and their own abilities.
Disorganized/ disoriented attachment 	The child does not have a strategy for how to react to people. It goes out to sea and returns to port without purpose or direction. It returns to other harbours. The child's ship appears to have been taken over by pirates, filling the ship with drama and confusion. These children have often experienced difficult relationships with their primary caregivers, and as a consequence, there is a tendency to focus on T (think trauma) when using the STORM model.	More than anything, the disorganized child needs a safe harbour with mentalizing, available, attentive, and helpful adults. As parents, you might experience intense emotions such as confusion, helplessness, anxiety, or anger. This means that you have a great need of help from other mentalizing adults to be able to maintain or re-establish your capacity for mentalization.

The lighthouse

As parents, you must act as a lighthouse for your child – a lighthouse which has a steady foundation and is not easily washed over, and a lighthouse which is able to see the big picture and which can throw a light on itself as well as the child.

The lighthouse is often used as a metaphor in psychology (Byrne 2016). In order to remember to be regulated, accountable, and mentalizing, you can use the acronym RAM. This is located at the top of the lighthouse, and above all, it is important that we keep this in mind when we interact with children.

> **R**egulated: Someone who is able to regulate themselves.
> **A**ccountable: Someone who can create a safe environment that encourages learning and development.
> **M**entalizing: Someone who is aware of their own and others' minds and see the child as an agent.

Suggestions and strategies

When times are hard, image yourself as your child's lighthouse. Be the adult who throws a light on your child, recognizes it, and is always regulated, accountable, and mentalizing.

Example

Fourteen-year-old Jessica posts an image on Instagram in which she is scantily dressed. Her mother is very upset when she sees the picture. Suddenly, she thinks that her daughter looks like a Playboy-model and she does not recognize her sweet little daughter. In the moment, the mother wants to tell her daughter off and yell at her that she has posted child pornography to the internet and that it can never be removed. But she is aware that in order to be her child's lighthouse she has to be regulated, accountable, and mentalizing.

The mother has a word with Jessica about the image. During their conversation, she holds on to the fact that, even though she is upset, it is her job to be *regulated*. She is also aware that these kinds of images can be seen by adults who have other intentions, and that she therefore has to be *accountable*. She must keep in mind that her daughter does not look at the image with an adult's eyes but simply tries to look like the models in the magazines, which the mother must attempt to *mentalize*.

MODEL **THE LIGHTHOUSE**

REGULATED   ACCOUNTABLE   MENTALIZING

Figure 2.4

How do you do it?

In order to become your child's lighthouse – the person who has authority and who your child wants to learn from – you need to work on letting your child know that you are someone who is worthy of *epistemic trust*:

Regulated

- Parents who inspire epistemic trust in their children are able to regulate their own emotions.

Accountable

- Parents who inspire epistemic trust in their children are able to re-establish and maintain their children's abilities to learn from others, take responsibility, and show direction.

Mentalizing

- Parents who inspire epistemic trust in their children are able to encourage their children to embrace new knowledge and learning, they know how the human mind works, and they keep a mental image of the child in which the child is able to meaningfully recognize itself.

The door to learning – epistemic trust

A child is ready to learn when the child trusts that the teacher – in this context, the parent – can teach it something that is personally relevant and generalizable for the child. Without this trust, it would be foolish to learn from him. He might teach the child something dangerous, for instance that blueberries are poisonous and that berries from a privet hedge are good to eat. From birth, children are ready to learn from their parents, but they are also able to be careful when the person who is supposed to be teaching them something does not seem dependable.

As a parent, you might lose the opportunity to teach your child something if you lose its trust. This could happen if you frighten or punish it, when what your child really needs is to learn how to regulate their emotions. You appear unreliable when you do not seem to be the one who is best able to teach your child something, when you are more frightened than the child in the face of danger, or when you get angrier than the child during conflicts.

Children need to learn, and they give their parents countless chances to become their teachers. They forget our mistakes and are ready to learn from us over and over again. So, even though you have taken a wrong turn, you have to get back on the horse and try to become the best teacher for your child.

Suggestions and strategies

In order to open the door to learning, you can use a few communicative tricks that stimulate the child's sense of being seen, acknowledged, and listened to, such as making eye contact with the child, actively using the child's name, making sure that your tone of voice is kind, and talking to the child in a manner where you, as a parent, are open and attentive towards your child's responses and questions (Bateman & Fonagy 2019).

Example

Twelve-year-old Ava is packing for an overnight excursion with her class. Ava yells: "I can't find my socks, and it's your fault. You're the world's worst mother!" Her mother becomes frustrated and says: "Don't talk to me that way." Ava keeps yelling: "I hate you!" Now, the mother tries to mentalize. A short while ago, Ava told her mother that she was really worried that no one would want to sleep with her. She said that they are all going to be sleeping in tents and that all the tents have already been filled, which means that she has to sleep in the same tent as two boys she doesn't like. Her mother wants to tell her that: "There will be no excursion for you if you speak to me like that." But instead she considers what is going on in Ava's mind and what she needs to learn. Ava is in need of strategies to regulate her emotions and to handle conflicts with her classmates. After having contemplated Ava's mind, the mother calmly asks her: "How would you feel if I talked to your teacher about how the tents are distributed?" Ava sits down on the floor and says: "Would you? I don't think I can find anyone who wants to sleep in the same tent as me."

MODEL **THE DOOR TO LEARNING**

Figure 2.5

How do you do it?

- Be available, regulated, accountable and mentalizing.
- Make sure that your child trusts you on a fundamental level.
- Inspire authority by helping the child make sense of what it is learning (see Figure 2.6). This makes you well-deserving of the power you hold over the child.
- Offer eye contact to the child. Use the child's name. Consider if your tone of voice is caring and talk to the child in a manner where you, as the parent, are open to and interested in its responses and questions.
- Be smarter.
- Regulate your emotions.
- Be Accountable. Create meaningful boundaries.
- Be Mentalizing towards your children.
- Always keep the door to learning open.

The lighthouse – giving and receiving authority

When children are born, they are far from being fully developed. There are entirely dependent on interaction with adults in order to survive and develop. For this reason, they are biologically predisposed for attaching to their parents. This means that biological parents have natural authority over their children. By being regulated, accountable, and mentalizing, parents retain this authority as the child grows up.

But what about stepparents, foster parents, or adoptive parents? In these cases, it is of vital importance for the child's development that the biological parents are willing to share their child and allow the child to subject itself to the other authority (allowing them to turn on the light in their lighthouse). As biological parents, therefore, you have an obligation to be supportive of your ex-partner, of the child's new stepparent, or of the child's foster parents. Otherwise you leave the child without opportunity for learning and development.

If you feel that a parent refuses to be supportive of your role as authority and attachment figure in a child's life, you must attempt to be mentalizing, even if you do not want to at first. One way of doing this is to remind yourself that when people meet you with anger, it is often a way of covering up vulnerable emotions such as hurt, grief, or anxiety. If you remember this, it might make it easier to mentalize. Sometimes it is simply not possible to establish a system of co-parenting that turns on the light in the lighthouse. If that is the case, you must try to turn on the light on your own by making a great effort with RAM.

Suggestions and strategies

If an authority/co-parent has not used their authority in an appropriate manner, it is necessary to acknowledge the child's experience, but at the same time it is important that you continually work on supporting your co-parents/authorities' (lighthouses) authority over the child (turning on the light).

Example

A stepmother relates how she experiences her stepdaughter, Anna, as a "trojan horse." Every time she returns from her biological mother, she vents about her stepmother's incompetence in furious terms. It sounds as if every word originates from her biological mother. In this case, the stepmother needs to turn on the part of the lighthouse that has to do with being regulated, accountable, and mentalizing. She must try to guess what has been going on in the mind of Anna's biological mother. Perhaps she is lonely, sitting by herself and missing Anna. Or perhaps she is hurt and angry that the person who has taken her husband and daughter from her is now the one who is having a good time with Anna. This helps the stepmother adhere to the fact that, despite Anna's behaviour and the contagious frustrations from the biological mother, she must stick to RAM in her role at stepmother.

MODEL GIVING AND RECEIVING AUTHORITY

Figure 2.6

How do you do it?

- Support the other primary teachers (lighthouses) in your child's life.
- Accept that children by nature have a hard time using teachers that have not been validated by those who have authority over them. This should lead to more mentalizing rather than anger, because mentalization begets mentalization.
- Be regulated, accountable, and mentalizing. This is the best way to gain authority when it is not naturally allocated to you.

Window of tolerance

The window of tolerance is inspired by Siegel's model of the same name (Siegel 2002). Everyone, children as well as adults, has a certain limit to the bodily signals and emotional intensity they are able to tolerate before mentalization breaks down.

When you are within the window of tolerance you are attentive and ready to learn and be present. When you are above the window of tolerance, you will experience intense emotions, bodily signals, and stimuli from the senses, for instance during an anxiety attack or an outburst of rage. In such cases, you might experience palpitation, shortness of breath, throbbing headache, and lack of control. Below the window, your mind is closed off, for example when you are asleep, recuperating, or shutting your mind to something, in which case you turn the energy inwards. This can be experienced as numbness.

Each individual's window of tolerance is different. Some people function most effectively at a high intensity, whereas others have a much narrower window, and more quickly feel overwhelmed. Naturally, it is easier to raise children who have a wider window or who are able to regulate themselves so that they are not pushed out of their window of tolerance. The size of a person's window of tolerance depends on their personality, experiences, and external influences such as stress, hunger, exhaustion, and mental strain.

Suggestions and strategies

When children are outside their window of tolerance, it is impossible to teach them anything. Start paying attention to the current state of your child's tolerance window – are they inside or outside their window? – and only create challenges for the child when you are within your own window of tolerance and when you are sure that you are able to challenge the child in an appropriate way.

The two following models, "Point of entry" and "Gangway," describe how you gain entry to the window of tolerance and how you work on expanding it.

Example

Three-month-old Eve is exhausted after her first session at a gymnastics class for new mothers and their babies. She cries and cannot be calmed down. When she finally falls asleep, she sleeps heavily and for so long that her parents are afraid that she has fallen into a state of unconsciousness, and they end up calling the doctor. Eve, however, wakes up in the middle of the conversation – happy, and with an open window of tolerance.

Three-year-old Peter is throwing a tantrum because he is not allowed to have candy before dinner. He spits on the floor. Of course, his mother will not accept this behaviour, even though he is angry. But she chooses to distract him first, asking him to go with her outside to light the candle in the Halloween pumpkin by the door. Afterwards, when Peter's emotions and bodily reactions are regulated and he has returned to his window of tolerance, it is possible for his mother to tell him that he is not allowed to spit on the floor.

Sixteen-year-old Kate has started hanging out with some of the "cool girls" at her school, and they have established a collective habit of being late for their classes. Kate's father has been informed, and he is determined to have a word with her about it immediately. But when he enters her room, he finds a girl who is exhausted after a football game and a long day at school. She has no energy, and it is clear to her father that she is not in a state where she has the necessary tolerance to listen and learn.

MODEL **WINDOW OF TOLERANCE**

Figure 2.7

How do you do it?

Be aware of your child's window of tolerance – is the window open, and is the child inside or outside its window?

- When the child's energy level is too high, learning is not possible.
- When the child's energy level is too low, learning is not possible.
- When the child is inside its window of tolerance, it is able to learn.

Point of entry

In order to enter into a social interaction with your child that encourages development and learning, it has to remain within the window of tolerance, and as a parent you must have developed your child's confidence in you, so that it feels that it is worthwhile to listen to you. But it is necessary that the child is mentally and physically available, and that it has the required level of tolerance. In other words, the ship must be in port when you want the child to learn something.

If you go on a boat cruise, there is a certain place where the ship sets out and lands again, and if you do not reach the boat in time, you must wait for the next trip. The same goes for children. Sometimes you must wait for the next departure and rely on the ship to return.

Suggestions and strategies

When it seems impossible to find a point of entry for interacting effectively with the child, it might be useful to do something nice together.

Example

Five-year-old Ella has suffered from an earache for some time. Her parents have not had a lot of time for her because the other two children in the family have required most of their attention. Her older sister has been hospitalized with appendicitis, and her older brother has been having a hard time at school and has needed a lot of support. Ella has a quick temper and has been involved in a lot of conflicts, at home as well as at her kindergarten. Her mother wants to sit down to tell her that she understands that things are a little hard for her at the moment. But every time she tries to talk to her, Ella says: "Be quiet!"

One day, as they are playing with some of Ella's toy animals together, Ella says: "I'm the little annoying monkey who teases the two cats, and I feel sorry for the two cats that they know the bad monkey." Her mother says: "I think the monkey's mother has been busy looking after the cats, because they have been having a hard time." She picks up a toy bear and continues: "Now, this is the mother, and she hugs the monkey to comfort it." Ella says: "What about the cats?" The mother replies: "Of course, the monkey-mother is going to be there for them too, but she needs to remember her little monkey as well." After they are done playing, Ella seems happier, and her mother wonders if she has found the point of entry to talk to Ella about the family situation.

MODEL **POINT OF ENTRY**

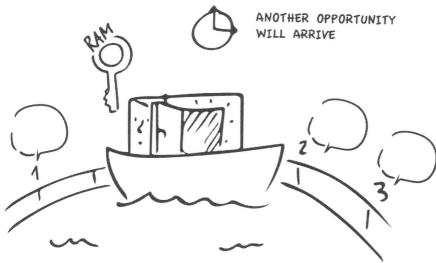

Figure 2.8

How do you do it?

- Is there a point of entry for learning?
- Make sure that your child is ready to learn.
- Pick your battles.
- It is a good idea to use shared activities as points of entry (car rides, walks, peeling potatoes).
- Make sure that the mirror neurons are not over-activated.

The gangway

The gangway to the ship is essential when it comes to teaching your child mentalization and self-regulation (cf. the intervention spectrum, Bateman & Fonagy 2007). The gangway is useful when the child is experiencing intense emotions or is outside their window of tolerance, that is when they are angry, scared or sad and do not behave in a mentalizing way.

Basically, you follow the child and walk back and forth across the gangway whilst adjusting what you say and do to the child's emotional intensity and mentalizing ability (Allen et al. 2010). The problem is that when you experience high emotional intensity, the ability to mentalize is diminished – and vice versa. This means that you cannot teach children anything about mental states when their emotions are running high.

The gangway has four steps. The first step is to *acknowledge and support the child's emotions*. The second step is to *explore* what has happened. The third step is when you step onto the boat and are able to talk about the *mental states of the people involved*. When you are on board the ship, you are sometimes able to *generalize mentalization* and talk about patterns of interaction, for example by verbalizing what is happen between you. You are seldom able to reach this last step in everyday life.

Suggestions and strategies

It is advisable to pay more attention to the child's emotional intensity and ability to mentalize than its behaviour. When the child's emotional intensity is at its height, you must be aware that the child is unable to mentalize. At this point, you simply need to support the child and try to understand, for example by saying: "I know how you feel. Sometimes I also get angry when I think something is unfair."

Example

Finn, who is almost 3 years old, throws violent tantrums. During these tantrums, he might bite other children, particularly his older brother. At first, his mother and father react by scolding and punishing him. But his tantrums keep getting worse and more violent. After that, the parents start using the gangway.

One day, as Finn pulls his brother Sean's hair because he wants the teddy bear Sean is holding, the father separates them and sits down next to Finn. Keeping pace with Finn's emotional intensity, he proceeds to carefully walk back and forth across the gangway: "Did you get upset because you couldn't have the teddy bear?" (acknowledge and support). This lowers the intensity of Finn's anger a little, and the father asks: "What happened? Was it because Sean had the teddy bear and you feel that it belongs mostly to you?" (explore). Finn gets angry and tugs at the teddy bear which Sean is hugging closely.

The father takes a step back on the gangway: "Did it upset you just now when you remembered the teddy bear, because you want to have it?" (acknowledge and support). "You wanted the teddy bear so much that you bit Sean?" (explore). Now, the father has almost reached the end of the gangway. "I know that it upset you but look at Sean. He was just watching TV, having a nice time with the teddy bear. How do you think it made him feel when you came and started pulling at it?" Finn now says that he is sorry and strokes his brother's hair (mentalization). That afternoon, Finn and his father are playing with Lego, pretending that one of the little figures is hitting the others. Together, they discuss how you might hurt others by hitting them if you are upset about something, and that it is much better to talk to someone about why you are upset (general mentalization).

MODEL THE GANGWAY

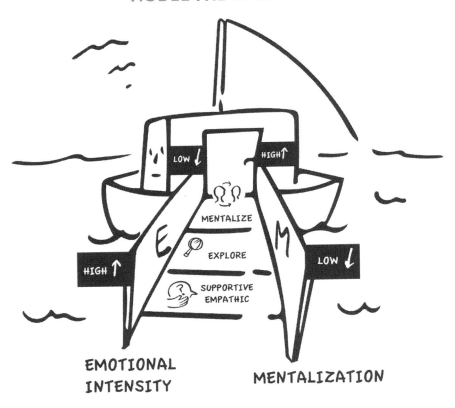

Figure 2.9

How do you do it?

- Step 1: Acknowledge and support
  - Acknowledge those emotions the child might be feeling.
  - Be supportive, respectful, and sincere.

- Step 2: Explore
  - Be genuinely curious when exploring the reason for the child's behaviour.
  - Reconstruct the situation.
  - Help the child make sense of their behaviour.
  - Find out which emotions lie at the root of the behaviour.

- Step 3: Mentalize
  - The perspectives of others are brought into the conversation.

- Step 4: Generalized mentalization

  - Look for patterns of reaction.
  - Talk about how these patterns unfold between your child and others.

I´ve noticed, that

- When you get upset, you want to hit someone, or

- When you are disappointed, you withdraw.

- When you need contact, you get angry.

When we cross the gangway to the child, we show the child that: I am here. I want to understand you. Even if I do not agree with you, I want to know how your feel.

Be proactive and think ahead

Natural forces are strong, and sometimes they seem insurmountable. This also applies to your child's most difficult developmental challenges. As a parent, you can feel powerless and overwhelmed. Usually, however, you get plenty of chances to revisit the same difficult situation. Three-year-olds who throw temper tantrums in social situations seldomly do it just once.

As a grown-up, you are able to take a comprehensive view of the situation, and you are not restricted to the present moment in the same way that a child is. As a parent, you need to practice staying in your lighthouse and using your ability to assess the situation and to mentalize. Be curious and explorative when a difficult situation arises. When does it happen? What makes your child react this way? How do you react? Do you have experience with doing something else?

Try to transform difficult situations into interesting and educational challenges. Consider them a part of the sea voyage. Those situations where everything seems the darkest are also full of potential for you and your child to grow – just like in adventures.

Suggestions and strategies

In those situations that often go wrong it is particularly important to be attentive and plan ahead. Keep an eye out for situations that are affected by tiredness, hunger, stress, loneliness, and anger. In such situations it can be a good idea to say: "We are leaving in five minutes" or "If you start to read now, then we'll read the rest together as your bedtime story." Give the child an apple before going shopping. Place a small plate with slices of fruit in front of the child who will likely be hungry soon. Put out the child's clothes the night before.

Example

A family who has a 3-year-old boy Simon and a 15-year-old girl Julia often experience conflicts in the morning. As a result, the mother and father are almost always late for work, and the family part on bad terms.

The parents start to look at their mornings from the outside. They see that the conflicts often have to do with whether Julia should bring a packed lunch to school or get lunch money. The conflicts often arise because Julia does not have time to prepare her lunch, and her parents usually do not have cash for the school cafeteria.

Every day, the mother drives Simon to his kindergarten, but it seems as if the conflicts with the older sister makes it harder to say goodbye, and it often ends in tears. The family comes to an agreement that if Julia prepares her lunch from home the two first days of the week, she can have money for the cafeteria the last three days. They pick up two rolls of coins at the bank to be used as lunch money. They agree that the father should start dropping off Simon at his kindergarten and arrange to evaluate these changes after two weeks at a family meeting.

MODEL **BE PROACTIVE AND THINK AHEAD**

Figure 2.10

How do you do it?

- Observe your own behaviour as well as the child's.
- Think ahead.
- Come up with ideas in peacetime that can help you avoid impending conflicts.
- Talk to other adults that are part of the child's life about what works well and what does not.
- Reflect on the situation with the child.
- Make agreements and set up rules in times of peace.
- Pay particular attention to situations that are affected by:
  - tiredness
  - hunger
  - stress
  - changes from one activity to another
  - feeling lonely
  - mentalization failure

On page 170 you will find a plan to be used in times of crisis which provides you with inspiration for reflecting on and perhaps planning what to do the next time you find yourself in a crisis.

Selective attention

Parents are able to actively direct their attention. Where they turn their attention has importance for their child, so it is important that parents are aware of what they direct their attention to. The metaphor of the lighthouse makes it easy to imagine how you can shine a light on positive behaviour. In general, it is encouraging for children that adults turn their attention towards them, see them, and shine a light on them.

Through this light you can guide your children. For example, you could be a role model for "less screen time" by putting your phone away at the dinner table or when your child is telling you something. Your attention can easily wander in many different directions, for example to your job, colleagues, your partner, or the dishes. But remember to turn your full attention to your child from time to time.

You can also actively use your attention in conflicts by momentarily disengaging it. For example, if you have had a dispute with your child about whether or not they should be allowed to have ice cream, and you have acknowledged the child's feelings, it can be a good idea to direct your attention somewhere else for a while, because if you continue to keep eye contact with the child, it will assume that the discussion is not over. By directing your attention somewhere else, you signal to the child that you are not having a dispute any more.

Suggestions and strategies

Children might feel that negative attention in the form of criticism and being told off is better than no attention at all. If your child has a tendency to behave inappropriately, consider if it is possible that the child experiences negative attention as a positive thing and therefore seeks to provoke it. Be attentive to your child when you want to encourage a certain behaviour.

Example

Fred's father is sitting at the couch with his iPad, busy checking football results. A few moments ago, he had a dispute with Fred, who wanted to wear his new snowsuit inside the house. The father had already spent time explaining to Fred that it is too warm to wear inside. Finally, he shifted his attention away from the conflict and put the snowsuit away. Fred stopped his protests and returned angrily to his room. Now, the father can hear the clattering of toy bricks in the hall. He gets up and goes to see what is going on. He finds his son, who has knocked over the box of LEGO bricks, spreading bricks all over the floor. The father spends a moment taking in the scene and contemplates that he has been available and paid positive attention to Fred for the past week. Then he says: "Cool, can I play? You have to show me how to build the greatest police station."

MODEL **SELECTIVE ATTENTION**

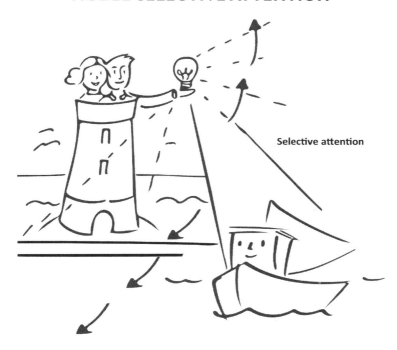

Selective attention

Figure 2.11

How do you do it?

- See your child and shine a light on it.
- Shine a light on the behaviour you approve of.
- Remove the light when a conflict is over, and signal that the topic is not in the spotlight anymore.
- Shift your attention elsewhere for a short while when you want to regulate your child.

Developmental path – from internal to external regulation

The child continually enters into new zones of development. The child develops from needing external regulation from its parents – over being able to self-regulate with support – and finally becomes internally regulated. When the child has to master new zones of development, parents must walk the fine line between supporting, challenging, and letting go of the child. Furthermore, they must be aware of the child's current developmental state, so they do not set expectations for the child that it cannot possibly live up to.

When observing the child's zone of proximal development (Vygotsky 1962), parents can either protect, make demands, or respect independence. This ability to understand what the child needs at its current developmental level is relevant throughout its childhood, from the child who has just learned to walk and who runs towards the stairs and starts to climb them, to the teenager who storms out the door with a bottle of vodka on a Friday night, headed for a party. Where is the child going here? Do they need protection or support, or are they able to fully master the situation? As parents, your job is to make sure that the child continues to challenge and test themselves. This requires great flexibility from the parents, because child development does not follow a linear path. Learned skills can suddenly fail. At other times, the child can make giant strides.

Suggestions and strategies

Take a look at the model on the next page and think about it as slowly slacking the rope for a boat. Little by little, you let go of a bit of rope until the child is able to act on their own – driven by inner values. Some classic examples are the ability to determine for yourself how much clothes to wear so that you feel neither too hot or too cold, how much you should eat before you feel full, or if something is dangerous. But in reality, the model applies to development in general.

Example

Two-month-old Josh is sitting in his mother's lap while she is talking to a friend. Suddenly the friend sneezes loudly. Josh is really scared by this, and his small body starts to shake. His mother comforts him by using a soothing tone of voice and gently hugging him, which calms him down. His mother tells him: "She just sneezed. It wasn't dangerous." Josh cannot regulate his anxiety on his own, but his mother can help him do this by protecting him (external regulation).

One night, when Josh is 4 years old, he is convinced that there is a man lying under his bed. He gets scared, but he is now so internally regulated that he is able to run to his mother, but then he starts to cry and sobs when he tells her that there is someone under his bed. The mother comforts Josh, and then they go to his room to look under the bed together. Josh is learning how to regulate his emotions. He is able to make use of his tool for emotion regulation – his mother – before he lets himself be overwhelmed by anxiety. Josh is almost able to self-regulate his emotions, but he still needs support.

When Josh is 15 years old, he is visiting Kate, whom he has a crush on. They are watching a horror movie together. Josh gets really scared, but he is able to regulate his anxiety. Kate, on the other hand, seems to need someone to hold her hand. Josh is now able to regulate himself, and even support Kate.

MODEL DEVELOPMENTAL PATH – FROM EXTERNAL TO INTERNAL REGULATION

External regulation	Zone of proximal development – self-regulation with support	Internal regulation
Is unable to do it alone. Needs protection or needs someone to help them through the situation.	Is almost able to do it alone. Needs attentiveness and participation.	Is able to do it alone. Independence is respected.

Figure 2.12

How do you do it?

- Always support the child's development from external to internal regulation.
- Is the child unable to do it alone? Is the child able to do it with support? Is the child able to do it alone?

- Take a critical look at yourselves as parents. Are you the kind of parents who overestimate your child's abilities and set them tasks at which they are bound to fail, or are you the kind of parents who do not pay attention to your child's current level of development and who keep helping the child, even when they are able to do it with support or even with no help at all?
- Accept your child's independence when they are able to do it alone – even if they sometimes make mistakes.

Chaos and rigidity – flexibility and mentalization

When bringing up a child, one has to walk a fine line between flexibility/chaos on the one hand and boundaries/rigidity and behaviour regulation on the other hand. Children (especially children with difficulties) need structure, guidelines, and boundaries, but they also need liveliness, flexibility, and moments of feeling seen and met by their parents. The secret is to stay in the middle of the "river" (Siegel & Bryson 2014) so that you do not allow too much chaos and flexibility but also do not become too rigid and focused on regulating behaviour. Teaching children to become well-rounded, well-functioning people who exhibit appropriate, culturally well-adapted behaviour and who have a well-established ability to mentalize is the continuous struggle of parenthood.

Figure 2.13 illustrates the dilemma you face as a caregiver when you sail down the river and attempt to stay in the middle between chaos on one river-bank and rigidity on the other. Some caregivers are too close to one bank, and the model can help them understanding the importance of getting closer to the other bank in order to support their children's development.

Suggestions and strategies

In some families, each riverbank is represented by different people. The father might represent the rigid approach to parenting that focuses on setting boundaries, while the mother represents the more flexible, gentle, and chaotic approach. If parents have positioned themselves on either side of the river, the model can be used to start a mentalizing conversation about how each river-bank represents an important element of parenthood.

Example

Mason loves to play computer games. He is 11 years old, and his parents think it is starting to take up too much of his time, keeping him away from other things that used to bring him joy. For instance, he would rather go home to play computer than to the youth club with his friends, and he is spending less and less time with the boy next door. When asked to turn off the computer, he drags it out and has to be asked again and again. When the computer is finally turned off, he goes to the bathroom to play on his phone.

Mason's father likes to play computer games himself, and he knows that you can get suspended if you log out in the middle of an online game, so he is not good at standing firm on the agreements made by the mother. Instead, the father often ends up so absorbed in the game that he encourages Mason to play just one more game. Mason's mother does not think Mason should be allowed to play at all, and the parents often end up on opposite sides of the river. It helps them to use the model to catch sight of the dilemma in their parenting rather than focusing on each other's shortcomings.

MODEL CHAOS AND RIGIDITY – FLEXIBILITY AND MENTALIZATION AUTHORS ADAPTATION

Figure 2.13

How do you do it?

In order to create a balance where you maintain flexibility and mentalization and avoid running aground in either rigidity or chaos, you must:

- Set boundaries but allow chaos and development too.
- Take a trip to the other side of the river if the parents have set up camp on either side of it.

Emotional compass for parental navigation

Emotions can be seen as our inner compass that helps us realize what is right and wrong and guides us. If we do not learn to understand our emotions, we end up without direction. There are no emotions that are better than others – we need all of them – not just happiness. In order to motivate children to verbalize their emotions it is necessary to understand what the different emotions mean and to create an environment in which there is a focus on emotions.

As parents, you teach your children about emotions by showing them that parents have different emotions. It is a good idea to be transparent about your emotions. Use your emotional compass to determine what is right for you as a parent – and what your child needs. We need to use our emotions, but in order to use them appropriately, we have to regulate them. If we use them without regulating them, it creates chaos and can frighten the child.

Basic emotions help us to:

- Become aware of what we like and what is important to us (joy).
- Connect with and listen to others (acceptance).
- Watch out for danger and react expediently (fear).
- Shift our attention (surprise).
- Take care of ourselves and sense when someone crosses the line (anger).
- Regulate ourselves – for example, crying releases endorphins, which raises our spirits. It makes us feel that something is important to us and that it hurts to lose it (sadness).
- Sense instinctively that something is not good for me or my child (disgust).

Suggestions and strategies

Emotions can trick you. They might be a part of your personal history in relation to something you are experiencing right now in your own life or to something that has happened at an earlier point in time. Because of this, it is important to reflect on the origins of your emotional reactions – and to be able to regulate them so that they are not more intense than the child's.

It is a good idea to calibrate your emotional compass to determine if it has been adjusted correctly. During your own childhood, you might perhaps have learned that it is not okay to feel curious, that anger is a bad emotion, or that one should not trust people outside of one's close family – these are examples of values that have been tied up with emotions, and therefore you might unknowingly pass them on to the next generation if you do not review and calibrate your emotional compass.

Example

Seven-year-old Carl has started walking to school with a friend every morning. They meet in the driveway and then walk to school together. Sometimes Carl oversleeps, and his friend has to wait for him. Carl appears entirely unmoved by this, but the mother gets angry (senses her own boundaries), and this encourages her to have a serious word with Carl about how it is not okay to treat others that way.

MODEL **EMOTIONAL COMPASS FOR PARENTAL NAVIGATION**

You have to help your child's notions become categorized emotions

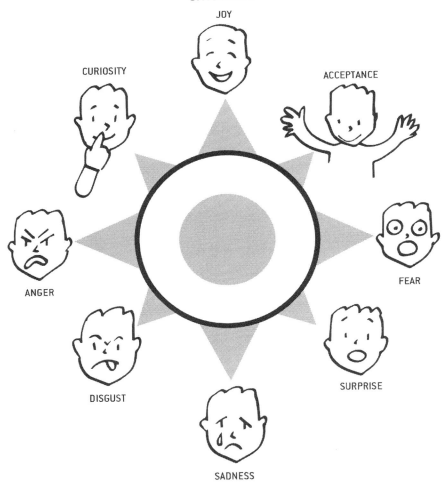

You have to help your child notions become categorized emotions

Figure 2.14

How do you do it?

- Use your emotional compass to determine what feels right for you as a parent.
- Listen to your emotions but regulate them.
- Make sure that your emotional compass is well-calibrated.
- Use your emotional compass in relation to your child. See page 144.

Anchor

A central feature of child development is learning emotional self-regulation. This process requires parents to focus on regulating their own emotions when their child is experiencing intense emotions. Then, when they are in control of their own emotional expression, they are able to support the child through its intense emotional experience.

Formerly, it was sometimes seen as good parenting to think: "When the child's emotions are intense – it's an offense." Today, however, parents should rather remember the words: "When the child is experiencing intense emotions and thoughts, that's when you should be their anchor." Children can learn to regulate themselves for fear of punishment, but this will not teach them emotional self-regulation. Rather, that ability is learned slowly through interaction with more mature, well-regulated minds.

The process of learning emotional self-regulation begins with the newborn child and continues throughout their childhood in different versions and with varying intensity. At any age, there is plenty for the child to learn when they come into contact with intense emotions.

Suggestions and strategies

It can be difficult to support emotional self-regulation without being contaminated by the unregulated emotions, but remember that a situation where your child is experiencing intense emotions is a great learning opportunity for you and your child.

Even though you are your child's anchor, this does not mean that you always have yield. Parents who often give in tend to experience more conflicts.

Example

Henry, who is 2-and-a-half years old, often has temper tantrums, which frustrates his mother. She has been told that she can teach him that it is not okay for him to get so angry that he kicks and breaks things. Her friend has told her that she can do it by giving him a timeout until he has calmed down. At first, she tries to confine him to his room, but she feels that this is too harsh. Henry screams and yells and is unable to calm himself.

Instead, she decides to just sit next to him when his feelings become too intense. That way, she can focus on calming herself down first and then help him do the same. When she sees how hard it is for Henry to calm himself down and how much it helps him to have her there as a calm presence, she feels ashamed to have left him alone before with emotions that are too intense for him to regulate on his own.

MODEL **ANCHOR**

**When the child's feelings are
intense – be an anchor and try
to make sense**

Figure 2.15

How do you do it?

You become your child's anchor and help them regulate their emotions when
you:

- Regulate your own emotions first.
- Know your strategies for emotion regulation (see p. 132).
- Are curious to discover the reason for your child's intense emotions.
- Distract them first if your child's emotions are very intense.
- Remember that experiencing intense emotions that lead to violent tan-
  trums are completely normal:

  - Age 1: 7.5 per week, averaging 2.1 min.
  - Age 2: 8.7 per week, averaging 3.9 min.
  - Age 3: 6.1 per week, averaging 4.2 min.
  - Age 4: 4.8 per week, averaging 5.0 min.

(Potegal & Davidson 2003)

STORM

The STORM-model contains all of the central elements that you should be aware of regarding traumatized children (Hagelquist 2012). The acronym STORM stands for security, trauma focus, obtaining skills, resource/strength focus, and mentalization. The word STORM can be seen as a symbol of the field you are working in when you are taking care of traumatized children and adolescents. It is a field full of energy and power. The storm can be a constructive force: cleaning up, stimulating development, and creating new opportunities and balance. But it can also be destructive and dangerous.

When it comes to child development, it is necessary for the child to have a safe and mentalizing environment. This is even more important for traumatized children. For children, developing skills and abilities is a central and natural part of social interaction, but if they do not feel secure, the child will concentrate its energy on avoiding danger rather than developing new abilities.

Suggestions and strategies

If a child has been living in a traumatic environment for an extended period of time, for instance because of a long illness or if an adopted or foster child has repeatedly been subjected to traumatic experiences, it will often have consequences for the development of the child's skill set. You must take the child's current developmental level as your starting point rather than evaluating them against what is typical for their age.

Example

On his way home from a friend's house, 11-year-old Aaron is held up by a man who threatens him with a knife and robs him of his phone. After this incident, he is afraid to leave the house and to be home alone. His parents stay close to him for a while. They pick him up from school, and the first couple of days he sleeps in their bed (security). Aaron has always had a tendency to be cautious and worry too much, so for a period of time his parents had encouraged him to leave his comfort zone a little, for example by having a sleepover at a friend's house, but after the incident they decide that this is not the time to push him (mentalization). They tell him that it is normal to avoid something that has scared you (trauma focus). The parents emphasize that Aaron did the right thing in the situation, both regarding the mugger and the police (resource/strength focus). When some time has passed to distance Aaron from the experience, they start to encourage him once again to experiment with his relations and stay over at a friend's house (obtaining skills and building relationships).

MODEL **STORM**

Figure 2.16

How do you do it?

Security

Security is a prerequisite for the child to be able to spend its resources on development rather than simply survival. Establish a safe environment that protects against new trauma but which also forms a safe space in the child's everyday life and ensures a good and secure contact with its parents.

Trauma focus

The child's behaviour might be a post reaction to a traumatic experience. Gather information about typical after-effects of trauma, pay attention to these reactions, and educate the child about them.

Obtain skills

Living in an environment that enables the child to focus on development rather than survival encourages the child to acquire skills that have not yet been properly developed.

Resource/strength focus

The child is encouraged to see its own unexplored resources and strengths even in relation to the traumatic event, which will make the child develop a more positive self-image. Resources or strengths should be understood broadly as inherent talents, qualities, personal characteristics, and coping strategies.

Mentalization

It is important to hold on to mentalization when interacting with the child, but also in relation to one's partner and social network.

Chapter 3

The child's development

It is both rewarding and joyful to see a child develop and acquire new abilities, but with new maturity comes new challenges. At any new developmental stage there will be advantages and disadvantages, and as parents, it is important not to focus only on the disadvantages but to also appreciate the advantages. It can be a source of frustration that development does not only move forward but sometimes involve regressions and that the path of development often alternates between good and bad patches (Illg & Ames 1967). It is important to be patient with development and always focus on what is normal.

Human children are born with underdeveloped brains that take up to 20 years to become fully developed. The brain is the only organ that is externally regulated through interaction with parents and the environment around the child. The newborn child has inherent potentials and capacities which unfold as the child develops, but in order for this to happen, the child must be met by mature adults who are able to support the child's development through interaction. Fortunately, parents are predisposed to offer their children an interaction that encourages development, but they also need to have a general knowledge about child development.

The better you know your child, and the more you know about what is normal, the better you are able to meet your child in a mentalizing way and thereby supporting its development. If we continue to use the ship as a metaphor for the child, you could say that the cargo is full of potentials, but that these potentials need to be cultivated, supported, and recognized in order to develop. The child's six cargo holds contain emotions, behaviour, social relations, physical development, self, and attention/cognition. According to psychologist Bessel van der Kolk (2005), these are the areas that normal children need to develop in their interaction with adults and other children.

In the following, each of these areas will be described in more detail in relation to the developmental phases of age 0–3, age 9–12, and age 13–18. Each description will be followed by a table that outlines the development that happens in that particular phase and how to support development in that phase, as well as how the ability for mentalization develops in that phase. These tables are meant as an inspiration, not as an instruction. The most important thing is to relate to each individual child.

Development age 0–3

Having a child is an enormous change in a person's life and it can feel like a huge responsibility. There is so much the child needs to learn and develop, and this makes most parents feel overwhelmed and uncertain sometimes. The change from being a family of two to one of three (or from three to four) is a major transformation. Putting another person's needs in front of your own requires energy, but it is necessary to be aware of because it lays the groundwork for becoming a safe harbour for a small child.

Luckily, there are plenty of spontaneous and instinctive reactions that support and help us in this process, but this is not to say that it is easy, for there are intense emotions and confusing processes involved. We draw on our experiences from our own childhood and the way we were treated, both consciously and unconsciously.

When reading the table mapping out the child's development from age 0–3, you should keep in mind that the period from age 0–1 is the time in a person's life where they develop the most. Pay attention to the child's signals. Be confident that your instinctive reactions – making noises, playing little games, touching and moving your child – play an important part in your child's development. Be careful not to overstimulate your child. When the child withdraws, it might be because it needs a small break.

The hardest part for parents in this period of the child's life is often worrying if you're are good enough to support the child's development. It can also be frustrating that the child needs time to perfect the abilities it has recently acquired. Perhaps the child has just said "Mum" for the first time, but then does not say it for days afterwards, or it has taken its first steps on Monday, but will not try again until the following week.

Suggestions and strategies

Little children need to learn many things through their interaction with their caregivers. But it is also a big part of the child's development that this progresses as naturally as possible, as long as the child receives the right amount of care and support. For this reason, it is important that you also learn to relax and enjoy your child – that way, things will happen in a much more natural way.

Example

A mother wants to support her little daughter's development. She takes such great care to name all of the child's emotions and help her understand how her body works that she sometimes forgets to enjoy everything that is happening between them. When the child's father comes home, she always says: "Please take her."

When the girl is almost 1 year old, she says her first real word. It happens one day as her father returns home from work, and the girl is so happy to see him that she exclaims what she thinks is her fathers "name": "Take-her!" The mother cannot stop herself from laughing, having spent so much time trying to teach her daughter to say "Mum."

MODEL DEVELOPMENT AGE 0–3

Figure 3.1

Emotions

The newborn child experiences basic emotions, but he has to learn how to register, categorize, and verbalize emotions through interaction with his parents.

When something wet comes out of the eyes and the child feels his body become heavy, he has to learn to register and categorize these signals as "sadness." Later, the child needs to learn to verbalize these signals as "I am sad."

Both the child and his parents are ready to enter into an interaction that promotes development in which the child's emotions are recognized by his parents. The interaction between parents and child also teaches the child to regulate his emotions. When parents distract the child from a source of stress and encourages him to turn down the "emotional-volume," the child gradually learns how to regulate himself. From birth, emotional self-regulation is an important part of the child's learning process, but this is especially clear from his first year onwards, as temper tantrums featuring a hitting, screaming, kicking, and spitting child are common.

Behaviour

A young child is able to perform delayed imitations of adults' movements and facial expressions. During his first year, the child's behaviour is characterized by a keen interest in exploring the surrounding world. The child forms new experiences through repetition. The child possesses inherent potentials for development which prompt him to behave in a way that the parents must respect and stimulate.

It can be challenging to keep in mind that there is no deliberateness beneath the newborn child's actions – which means that telling him off or rationalizing with him has no effect. This makes heavy demands on the parents' tolerance and ability to accommodate the child. The child's behaviour directly communicates his emotions and experiences, and it is the parents' task to help the child regulate these inner states and put them into words.

Another challenge can be that the child has not yet developed certain abilities, such as cognitive or emotional abilities, and therefore might act in dangerous or socially unacceptable ways: such as biting or running away. The child's natural curiosity can also be a challenge, for instance when he eats dirt or runs into the street but remember that curiosity is the foundation for learning.

Learning to regulate emotions other than anger is similarly hard, for example when the child cries and is intensely sad at partings, or when he gets very afraid of a noise, of large things, of cars or dogs, or later in this period, of monsters and bogeymen under the bed.

Physical development

The child develops at a tremendous pace in this period, and constantly acquires new physical abilities. The newborn child has a body but is not yet familiar with it and does not know how to interpret bodily signals.

In this period, the child must learn to register, categorize, and verbalize bodily signals such as feeling hungry or full, hot or cold, tired or awake, as well as the sense of being in his own body.

For example, the child needs to learn to register (that was a fart, and it came from me), categorize (that is what a fart sounds like) and regulate (sometimes I am able to control when I fart).

The child gets to know his bodily states through physical and mental interaction. The skin cells on my hand registers touch. When these sensations are put into words and are mirrored, the child is familiarized with his bodily functions – does it tickle? Does your belly hurt? (physical). Did that feel cold? (mental).

Some children have a hard time regulating sleep, others hunger. Some easily feel overstimulated by physical contact, while others need physical contact all the time to feel secure.

When the child is around two-and-a-half years old, his newly developed independence manifests itself in the child's insistence on doing things himself.

Social relations

Right from birth, the child gains his first experiences with social relations. During his first interactions with adults, the child starts to form expectations about whether the world is a safe place or not, and whether he can depend on others to help satisfy his needs.

When the child experiences the caregiver as a safe harbour, he learns that it is worthwhile to seek contact and reach out.

This sense of security means that the child is able to spend his energy on exploring the world.

At the 8–12-month mark, the child starts to form a fixed conception about what he can expect in terms of patterns of attachment – that is, what he can expect from social relations. These patterns remain stable all the way into adulthood (see p. 48).

It is important to allow the father to become an important relation for the child (in his own way). Letting the child form a good and strong relationship with his father has a lot of positive effects, for the child as well as for the father and mother (see p. 75).

Self

The small child is a unique individual with competencies and potentials. The child develops and gets to know himself by interacting with dedicated adults. The child's ability to create a coherent sense of self depends on the experience of being perceived as a human being with a mind. The parents' ability to recognize the child's potentials and to conceptualize him as his own person is essential for the child to develop a sense of self. The parents' perception of the child influences the way they interact with the child, and the child develops his own sense of self through his parents' words, gestures, and tone of voice.

The child's sense of self consists of both an **I** and a **me** – the 'I' part of the self *does* things–I am so good that even when there is not much milk, I make an effort to suckle. The 'me' part of the self *is* things–I am daddy's sweet boy.

During the first year, the child starts to develop a sense of intentionality, and to experience himself as an individual who is able to actively engage with the world.

It can be challenging to respond appropriately to the 2 ½ year old child in relation to his particular sense of independence and the conflicts that this gives rise to. At this age, the child starts to develop a sense of shame, which can have the desirable function of curbing inappropriate behaviour, but needs to be balanced so that it can develop into guilt, which is a more appropriate emotion (see p. 218).

Attention/cognition

The development of **attention** is essential for the child, because it determines the kinds of information that is registered from the child's experiences.

From birth onwards, the child's attention develops gradually to become more controlled, adaptable, and planned.

Around 6–9 months, the child begins to refer to his caregivers to see how they respond to what is happening in the environment. For example, if the child sees a dog, he will look to his parents to see if it is safe (social reference). After the child reaches the 12-month mark, he not only participates in shared attention, but attempts to actively create shared attention by pointing to something and expect his parents to respond to what he has pointed out.

Cognition (thinking, knowledge and language, the ability to interpret and create meaning). The greatest strides in a person's life, in terms of development, are taken during the first years of life. Here, it can be a challenge to find the right balance between providing adequate stimulation and overstimulation.

Emotions

You have to help your child's notions become categorized emotions.

Take an interest in your child's emotions. Notice them and put them into words, preferably as questions: "Did you get scared?" "Did you think that was fun?" The way you use your voice, your posture, and your facial expressions when talking to your child helps the child to understand his emotions. When you talk, play, and react to your child's expressions, you are teaching your child something fundamental about emotions. Remember that no emotions are better than others and that they are all a part of your child's emotional compass.

The only way for your child to learn emotional self-regulation is if you act as a role model by regulating your own emotions.

When your child's feelings are intense – be an anchor and try to make sense.

In order to help your child regulate his emotions, you must regulate yourself first – then try to discover the reason for the emotions. If the emotions are very intense, then distract the child. Be proactive from a long-term perspective – in which situations does it happen?

Physical development

The child is in possession of a body and inner physical experiences, but it is through interaction with his parents that the child gets to know itself and regulate itself physically.

Behaviour

With a small child, you regulate his behaviour physically. When the child grabs your hair, your gently pry his hand loose and holds on to it. If it is time to sleep, you wrap the child in a blanket and rock him to sleep to accommodate the child's lack of motor regulation skills. During the first year, the primary task for the parent is to show engagement and participation through these physical regulations, thereby teaching the child that the world is a safe place, so that he learns others can assist his sense of "changing behaviour."

Later on, you start to use the toolbox where you acknowledge the child and set a direction: "You want to be nice to the dog, but it likes it best if you pet it like this." In this period, the child is unable to control his own actions or regulate himself simply through verbal instructions to stop what he is doing.

You regulate behaviour by looking beyond the behaviour and encouraging the child to do what you want him to do by indicating what it is. It is advisable to make careful and appropriate demands, so the child can develop.

Social relations

Let your child feel that you are there for him. Console, change diaper, play, tickle, laugh, and talk. Be a safe harbour from which the child can explore himself, and a safe base that he can return to.

Physical development

When you touch your child, you help him define the boundaries of his body from the surrounding world. The child senses contact between the skin cells on his back and your hand when you stroke him, and this registers in the child's brain, connecting his brain to his body.

Gently support regulation of the child's physical needs such as sleeping and eating. When you help your child regulate himself physically, you lay the foundation for physical self-regulation later on.

The dialogues and physical interactions you have with your child serve as practice for your child to learn to register, categorize, and verbalize physical states: "Are you hungry?" "Are your hands cold?" "Are you tired?"

Self

Help your child develop a positive self-image, by acknowledging him both as an active "**I**" as well as the wonderful person "**me**."

Support the child in constructing a coherent narrative about himself. Before the child is able to talk, tell him: "You are someone who is curious," "you are someone who is really making an effort to get milk out of the breast."

When your child starts to talk, tell him positive stories about himself, and help the child construct a life story – ask leading questions: "We went to the playground today and it was fun to see the donkey there, do you remember?"

Assist the child, who is in the independence phase, in understanding that it is possible to disagree and have conflicts without someone being wrong.

Social relations

If your child is a little too avoidant and does not use you when he feels insecure, you need to help him to want to seek comfort. Show your child that it is worthwhile, and that you want to understand him.

If your child is a little too ambivalent and almost does not dare to leave your side to explore the world, show the child that you have faith in him and believes that he is able to do it on his own.

If your child is affected by difficult early experiences and has no coping strategies, you should be especially mentalizing towards him, and remember to seek support from others – because this can be a very hard situation for you too.

It is good for the child to have many different types of relations – for example, to see that mom and dad do things differently. The child benefits from learning that you can be consoled, reprimanded, loved, or played with in different ways.

Attention/cognition

Having a sense of security allows the child to direct his attention away from his parents. The parents are involved in developing the child's attention by noticing the child's signals and keeping his attention focused on something for some time.

Work on finding a balance between stimulating the child and avoiding overstimulation.

The child learns the things he needs to know about the world from his caregiver – this applies to language, colours, names, and animal sounds, among other things. Teach your child as much as possible through playful interaction.

Self

Attention/cognition

When you set boundaries, position yourself physically on a level with the child. This helps calm the child down because you do not appear as intimidating. It makes the child feel safe when he knows what he is and is not allowed to do. That way, you strengthen his sense of being a positive, active self who is able to clearly set his personal boundaries.

Age	Mentalization	How do I support my child's mentalization?
0–6 months	The development of mentalization relies on interaction between child and parents, but it is primarily something that the parents teach the child by being mentalizing towards him. This means that they have a relevant hypothesis about what is going on in the child's mind. Through marked mirroring, the parents send the child's emotions and mental states back to him. This way, the child learns to understand them. Marked mirroring is when parents express their emotions in a slightly different way than the child, by which the parents indicate to the child that they are not expressing their own emotions, but rather that they are expressing emotions to help the child understand his own emotions. Through these interactions, the child develops a range of mental categories for emotions and states. This means that the child's mental categories for emotions are primarily based on his experiences with his parents.	The child develops his ability for mentalization by feeling secure and by interacting with mentalizing adults. Parents can encourage the development of mentalization in their children by being attuned to the child and by acknowledging the child's emotional expressions through empathic and marked mirroring. It is essential for the child to experience such interactions repeatedly. At the same time, it is important to remember to let the child rest when you notice that he is becoming overstimulated. Marked mirroring is something we do instinctively when we understand what is going on in the child, so there is no need to consciously make silly faces. Instead, you can spend your energy to try to understand what is happening in the child's mind – then the mirroring will happen automatically. It is important to verbalize what is going on in the parents' minds as well as the child's. Talk to and about the

Age	Mentalization	How do I support my child's mentalization?
		child in a mentalizing way. Use a motherese tone, use turn taking and treat the child as an agent. Refer to the child as an intentional person with emotions, thoughts, and desires — even before the child is able to express these things in words. Parents who are interested in exploring their own minds are more prone to take an interest in their child's mind.
6 months	When the child is around six months, he starts to notice causal relations and becomes able to connect behaviour with the agent behind the behaviour. From six months onwards, the child is able to understand that animals are autonomous and different from mechanical things.	Support the child's emerging understanding of causality between what is happening in the other person's mind and what the other person does. Put various mental states into words using figures in cartoons, books, animals, toys etc.
8–12 months	The child begins to understand that when his parents do something, they do so based on an intention. The child also begins to expect his parents to act rationally and he is able to understand that there are intentions behind his own behaviour and that he can choose between different possible lines of action (should I crawl or push myself forward on my tummy, which is faster?). The child is still unable to	The parent can help the child connect the physical world with his inner world so that the child understands the relation between them. "Mom is just going to the kitchen to pick up your porridge." Subtitle your own mental states: "Mom got scared, that is why she yelled." Connect the mental with the physical, for instance by saying "Mom loves you" while giving the child a kiss.

Age	Mentalization	How do I support my child's mentalization?
	appreciate mental states and is limited to what he can see. So, if mom has gone to check on the child's twin in the other room, the child cannot understand what her intention is, because he cannot see her. The child does not yet fully understand that his own inner world is private and individual, because he has learned to understand this inner world through his parents.	
15 months–3 years	The child starts to develop a language for mental states and becomes able to act on and think about others' emotions and needs in a non-egoistical way. The child begins to understand that people are intentional, and he is now able to distinguish between the intentional goal of a behaviour and the random consequences of that behaviour. During the second year of the child's life, he starts to develop the ability to perceive that others experience the same mental states as he does (psychic equivalence) and he starts to play with mental states that he is not experiencing himself at that moment – for instance, when the child pretends that the baby is sad (pretend mode).	Help the child help others. Encourage him to share and remind the child of episodes where he experienced the pleasure of being acknowledged that way by others. Talk to the child about other children and adults' emotional expressions and outbursts. Propose interpretations and guesses about the reason why he became so angry, sad, scared, or happy. Connect this to the child's own experiences with the same or similar emotions so that the child starts to form mental images about what is going on inside other people's minds. Be aware of the fact that until they are four years old, small children are particularly in danger of having outbursts of anger and frustration

Age	Mentalization	How do I support my child's mentalization?
	These two abilities are the frontrunners of true mentalization. Most children at this age understand that other people's behaviour is influenced by their current mental states (thoughts and emotions) and of other more stable characteristics, such as abilities or personality.	because they expect others to know what they are thinking and feeling and that others feel and experience situations in the same way that they do. Encourage play, as it forms the basis of practicing mentalization.

Development age 4–8

During the period from age 4–8, the child develops from a preschooler to being well under way at school. Central developmental psychologists (Freud and Eriksson) refer to this as a period where the healthy child experiences mastery and initiative as well as cognitive development and development of a gender identity. This period usually begins with many challenges, but its ends with relative calmness and stability. The child becomes more preoccupied with other relations than the ones it has with its parents, and friends of their own age as well as other adults play an important part in the child's development.

Suggestions and strategies

During this period, the child acquires most of its knowledge through play. Consequently, it is very important to join the child in play (also ruff and tumble play), let the child control the game, and provide the child with the opportunity to play with children of the same age.

Example

A six-year-old boy is on his way home from soccer practice with his mother. He keeps challenging his mother to compete against him: "I'll race you to that tree!" His mother picks up speed a little, while the boy races ahead. When the mother reaches the tree, he concludes: "I am the fastest in the world. I am so cool" (omnipotence and sense of mastery). At bedtime, he boy teases his younger brother by calling him fat (new mentalization skills) and they end up fighting (experimenting with getting to know one's body/physical activity). When it is time to sleep, the boy is unable to calm down. He is afraid that his mother and father will die and leave him. He asks a thousand questions about where he will live if that happens. Will his mother promise him that it won't happen? He also wants to call his father, who is on night duty, to make sure he is alive (regulation of anxiety must be supported – with an honest response to the child).

MODEL DEVELOPMENT AGE 4–8

Figure 3.2

Emotions

At this age, the child develops the ability to categorize, verbalize, and regulate emotions, but he still needs support in all of these areas. He has an emerging understanding of self-conscious emotions such as guilt, embarrassment, and envy, as well as mixed emotions such as feeling sad and angry at the same time.

The child practices regulating the physical basis for emotional self-regulation independently, see below.

At the beginning of this period, the child has a hard time regulating outbursts of anger. The child still has not reached a developmental stage where he understands that there can be other perspectives on what he experiences than his own. Scientists have figured out that on average, 4-year-olds experience eight temper tantrums per week with an average duration of 5 minutes.

Some children need more support than others when it comes to regulating anxiety. When the child experiences anxiety it overwhelms him, and he feels convinced that what he is experiencing represents reality – *this is the way it always is.*

For the 6–8-year-old, unregulated anxiety can be directed towards more existential themes such as the fear that his parents will not come to pick him up, that his parents will die, or that there will be a terror attack.

Behaviour

The child is able to act independently and actively, and to succeed with his actions. This means that they develop a sense of mastery and a fundamental belief in his own ability.

When the child is around 5 years old, he is able to comply with his parents' guidelines by recalling them in similar situations and repeating it out loud to himself: "You are not supposed to cross the road without looking both ways first." Later, the thought alone is enough for the child to regulate his behaviour.

In terms of behaviour, at this stage, the child needs to learn what constitutes good social behaviour. The child is preoccupied with rules and is therefore also ready to learn social rules.

Around the age of 8, the child begins to understand that these rules are not universal, but that they are created by people and can be negotiated. The child remains interested in testing the boundaries of different adults.

During this period, the parents act as role models. The child looks at them to see how they handle emotions, social relations, and conflicts. Therefore, it is important that the parents are aware of their own behaviour.

The child often becomes more interested in gender specific behaviour – for example, that girls play dress-up with high heels and lipstick, and that boys are more likely to play with tools.

Physical development

At this age, the child develops a sense of mastery and competence when it comes to his body. He can improve his physical competencies through sports, which precisely requires him to have control over his body.

This period is relatively harmonious in terms of physical changes.

Through play (and especially ruff and tumble play), the child exercises the physical aspect of emotional self-regulation – during these games, the child experiments with first turning up the volume as far as it goes, and then turning it all the way down again – for instance, during the game dance freeze: when the music is playing you dance as wild as you can (vol. 10) but when the music stops you must freeze and stand as still as you can (vol. 0).

From the beginning of this phase, the child is curious about all body parts and erogenous zones. The child enjoys touching them, and it is particularly interesting to talk about and look at penises and vaginas – it is also normal for children at this age to engage in sexual games with children of the same age.

Self

The child experiences himself as competent and able to master the tasks before him, which supports the development of the self – the child experiences himself as an active I.

The child's self-worth and sense of being 'me' is affected by the fact that the child's inner life is becoming more and more nuanced. Increasingly, great importance is attached to the child's inner abilities and as well as the skills which the parents attribute and articulate to the child, but also the skills that are emphasized by teachers and friends. The child starts to assess his own worth and learns that these evaluations evoke certain emotions.

Social relations

In this period, the child develops more advanced social skills – from primarily playing with adults, the child now begins to play with other children of similar age in a more interactive role-playing games rather than parallel play. During these interactions, the child explores different versions of himself. He also begins to test other children's boundaries.

The child also increasingly seeks out other adults than his parents, such as teachers or kindergarten teachers. Because of the child's newly developed ability to conceal his inner states, he is now able to understand that others are unaware of what is happening inside his mind. It is therefore entirely normal for children at this age to experiment with lying, cheating, or manipulating others.

The child becomes aware of hierarchies – who is bigger, who is smaller, who should make the decisions? The child has more conflicts with children who are similar in age than with children who are younger or older, because there is a greater struggle for rank when it is unclear who should be in charge, because no one can claim natural leadership based on their age.

Attention/cognition

In this period, the scope of attention is constantly expanding. The child is able to remain focused on something for still longer periods of time, but he still cannot pay attention to more than one thing at a time.

The world is opening up for the child, and so is his understanding of it. Some children become extremely curious and might ask a lot of "inquisitive Tom"-questions about the world (some children ask up to 400 questions on average on a daily basis).

When they start school, some children have a highly positive view of their own abilities (omnipotence) but this trust in their abilities is an advantage because they are about to embark on

Self

It is characteristic for the preschool child and the child just starting school that he might have a very positive perception of himself and brag about his own fantastic abilities. This is a consequence of the child's developing sense of independence and mastery. Around the age of 8, inner references such as interests and values start to influence the child's self-concept. This way, the self becomes more stable.

Attention/cognition

a new and challenging part of their lives with schooling and learning. The child begins to understand that rules and norms are socially constructed between people, that they are based on agreement and morality, and that they can be negotiated.

The child can begin to understand abstract concepts such as left and right, but he is still at a stage where he understands the world in a tangible way, and it is hard for him to understand mindsets and concepts that refer to things he cannot see.

How do you support development from age 4–8?

Emotions

At this age, is it important to keep these two sentences in mind:

- When your child feelings are intense – try to be an anchor and make sense.
- You have to help your child notions become categorized emotions.

If your child is facing intense anxiety, talk about the emotion but be honest – children become more afraid if they cannot trust the adults. "We are all going to die, but it is very rare that parents die from their children." Try to challenge the anxiety but do it slowly to allow the child to experience control.

It can be a good idea to talk to the child about emotions, watch movies about emotions such as Disney Pixar's animated movie *Inside Out*. You can show the child the emotional compass and explain to them that emotions can be dialled up and down in the same way as a volume button. You can also talk to them about how emotions are like clouds – they come and go, and it is possible to simply watch them without engaging with them.

Physical development

The child is now able to control his body and wants to play, climb, and do sports. Encourage them to exercise their body as much as they are able to.
Be a part of the child's physical universe. Romp about with him,

Behaviour

It is important that the child experiences a sense of mastery rather than inadequacy or defeat. Assist the child in learning basic social rules: washing hands before dinner, how to greet people politely, not to waltz around the living room naked – be your child's patient teacher. Engage the child's inherent desire to learn, so that they are motivated by interest and curiosity – for instance, when he wants to help set the table, cook dinner, and so on.

It can be a good idea to set down some rules in the family about bedtime, morning routines, table manners, and screen time.

If you have created a set of rules, you must stick to them in situations where parents have to say no in a mentalizing way – children who experience parents that adhere to their decisions learn to refrain from the behaviour more quickly, which provides them with a predictable environment and dependable caregivers (see p. 228).

Be a role model of good behaviour. Present the child with different role models – for example, make sure that all of their role models are not based on the same gender.

Social relations

Help your child put his day at kindergarten/school in words. "Did anyone do something nice for you or for somebody else today?" "Did anything happen today that made you sad or angry?" "Who helped you/ talked to you?" "What was the

Physical development

show that you are interested in his interests, and do things together.

Be aware that the child is exercising the physical aspect of emotional self-regulation when he turns the physical and verbal aspects of the game up or down. Allow him to do this – if it takes up too much space, move the game outside – in order to learn how to self-regulate, you must practice.

The child is only able to talk about those parts of its body which have been given a name – children who are able to put things into words can seek help – both in cases of physical injury that require a doctor as well as in cases of sexual abuse. "A knowing child is a secure child."

Anything that exceeds the child's current level of development does not interest him, so do not be afraid to say too much.

As for sexual games between children, you should make sure that the children are of the same age, that they respect personal boundaries, and that threats and adult sexuality are not involved.

Social relations

best thing that happened today, and what was the worst thing?" By remembering their experiences, the child can learn to appreciate his own role in creating a good atmosphere. But be careful that you do not set your expectations too high when it comes to your child's relational and linguistic ability to describe these situations.

Support your child's relations to other children by helping them when they have difficulties. Use conflicts as an opportunity to teach the child basic relational skills. If a play session with another child has gone awry, you can explore what happened together: "What happened?" "Who started it?" "Did you take turns?" "Why did you stop playing?" "Who was there?"

Invite one of the child's friends over and arrange for them to have a successful experience, with your help. At home, you could, for instance, play out those situations that often go wrong. Teasing between siblings can be undesirable and annoying, but it is also an expression of the child's developing mentalization ability. The child knows which buttons to push and how best to tease his sibling – use these situations as learning opportunities, when you have the energy for it.

In terms of the child's relations to adults, continue to provide him with positive experiences through games, playing on the child's terms, and being silly together. The better the relation between parents and child, the better the relation between the child and his friends and siblings.

Self

Play with the child's sense of self by asking them to describe their own and others' personalities. The child's sense of self is still in the making, so do not expect too much. Pay attention to the child's positive behaviour and put it in words: "You are someone who keeps trying even when it is difficult."

Support the child's (sometimes) overrated sense of self-worth and self-confidence. Regulate it if it becomes too much but be careful, because omnipotence and independence are gifts that help move your child forward.

Since the child does not like to feel threatened by or detached from his parents, he will adjust his behaviour to their expectations.

Following situations where the child has experienced shame, it is important to focus on repair. When parents are able to quickly reconnect with the child, they form a tighter bond with him and show him that he is "good enough" and that his relation to his parents has not been damaged.

Attention/cognition

Stimulate your child's attention: How long is he able to sit still if you set him a task that is so interesting that he has to keep working on it for a little longer. The adult trains the child's attention by pointing, showing, conversing, and explaining.

Computer games and iPad are most stimulating for the child's development if there is an adult sitting next to them who provides information about the world and about social relations.

Help your child develop strategies for solving a difficult problem or a task through planning and dividing the problem into smaller parts to make it more manageable. The child still learns a lot from their parents at this age. Tell the child about the world: in the car, when you go for a walk, when you tug them in. It can be anything from car brands, how tractors work, or who the president is.

Inquisitive-Tom-children can be annoying but try to see your child's natural curiosity as a gift.

Read aloud to and with your child and encourage him to write. Introduce personal, meaningful topics to your conversations to inspire the child to listen and use their language in return.

Mentalization and the 4–8-year-old child

Age	Mentalization	How do I support my child's mentalization?
4 years	When the child is around four years old, it is his "mentalization graduation day." The proper mentalization ability has nearly been developed, based on the initial stages of mentalization. The ability to mentalize is far from fully developed, but the child begins to understand that other people's actions are based on beliefs, which are sometimes wrong. This graduation depends on both the child's genetical predisposition for mentalization as well as his interaction with the environment. The "graduation" means that the child: • Displays more empathic behaviour. • Experiments more with cheating and deception, because he realizes that you do not know the same things that he knows. • Shows a decrease in physical aggression because he understands why the other person acts the way that (s)he does, which helps him control his impulses. • Begins to comprehend the basis for misunderstandings. • Develops more positive social relations with children of the same age. • Prefers to play with other children rather than adults.	The child needs a safe and secure social context in order to celebrate his "mentalization graduation." Without a safe environment in which others express interest in the child and his mental states, there is a risk that the child develops a fragile mentalization ability that breaks down easily. It is not only parents who play an important role when it comes to optimizing the child's mentalization ability – other adults in the child's life do too. The child still gets frustrated sometimes, and even though the child has celebrated his "mentalization graduation" the ability is still not fully developed. For this reason, it is important that parents balance their expectations in relation to their child. When the child lies and cheats it is a reflection of healthy development. Of course, the parent should make a comment about it, but it is also important to remember that it is a healthy sign. Parents can help their child unfold misunderstandings and the conflicting emotions that they can elicit in the child.

Age	Mentalization	How do I support my child's mentalization?
		The child's newly developed mentalization ability is sustained through interaction with other children. It motivates the child to see older children's skills in social situations. The child realizes that the older children have a better understanding of their own and others' minds, and that it gives them a higher position in the hierarchy. This is a motivational factor for the child to develop these skills himself. You can talk to the child about its development over time: "What were you like when you were little?" Look at pictures together and support the child's sense of being the same person over time.
8 years	The child begins to develop an image of himself that is stable over time. This is what constitutes a coherent sense of self. The child gains the experience that humans are able to influence social situations and he understands that his own and others' actions rely on beliefs, emotions, and needs.	The child begins to understand that his own or others' expectations can influence how ambiguous situations are interpreted. Here, it is important that parents help unfold misunderstandings as well as the conflicting emotions that can arise as a consequence of your own or others' choices, actions, and beliefs.

Development age 9–12

For many children, this is a relatively calm period in which they acquire new skills and are able to do a lot of things. At this age, the dominant theme is the newly developed abilities to social comparison and self-evaluation.

Among girls especially, these abilities form the basis of many conflicts and frustrations. This might be due to the fact that these abilities have been important in relation to the challenges that women have faced down through the ages. Evolutionarily speaking, women had to relate to the social hierarchy in villages and settlements to a larger extent than men, while also having to take care of the children – challenges that require abilities to perceive, understand, and compare social hierarchies.

Put in popular terms, girls start off by selecting who they want to play with before they decide on an activity. Boys, on the other hand, decide on an activity first and then they figure out who to play with. In this period, boys as well as girls explore close social relations and they can be very clear when it comes to excluding children they do not want to partake in the game. This way, they practice new competencies. As adults, we often have a few close friends and perhaps only one partner throughout our life. Therefore, we need to be able to choose healthy social relations and establish boundaries in a mature, caring, and respectful way. At this period, where the child practices establishing boundaries, it is in need of adults who talk to him about: How it appears from the other side. How messages are received and interpreted by others. How others receive the child's communications on the inside. How to deal with rejection.

Pre-adolescence is also on its way which leads to the first bodily changes and curiosity about how to handle one's sexuality and the opposite sex.

Suggestions and strategies

Be the mentalizing adult who is able to see the child from the outside. During this period, many conflicts can be established between different parents, and it is important that the adults lead the way when it comes to making social relations and groups work.

Example

A 12-year-old boy cannot sleep, so he gets up and goes to his mother. He tells her about school, where he is having some trouble with math, and about his best friend who did not want to hang out with him that day. Finally, he says that he misses his father, who is away travelling. His mother says: "You can sleep here, at your father's side of the bed." "I don't want to," says the boy, "because Dad has probably masturbated under the duvet." "I'm sure he hasn't," the mother replies.

"You don't think Dad has ever masturbated?" "Yes, I do, it's perfectly normal." "Do you think I'm ever going to masturbate?" "Yes, I think so." "How do you know when it is normal to do it?" "I think you just try it a bit and then see if it feels good." "Okay. Goodnight!"

MODEL DEVELOPMENT AGE 9–12

Figure 3.3

Emotions

The child's social relations with others are now largely characterized by dialogue rather than play. The previous stages of emotional development need to be completed before the child is able to engage in fruitful conversation with children of the same age.

At the age of 10, the child is more observing, tasting, and reflexive in relation to its own emotions. The child is now able to regulate her emotions.

The child is also able to use its understanding of other people to manipulate them – girls can almost seem cruel because they have a sophisticated understanding of how they can affect someone's emotions negatively.

Unregulated emotional outbursts no longer happen in public, but at home in a safe environment.

Physical development

The child has a good sense of its own body and of mastery over it. Throughout this period, its physical skills improve through sports or other physical activities.

At the same time, puberty begins, where some children develop faster than others, and this requires a balance in relation to the other domains – emotional self-regulation and social relations.

The first physical signs of puberty for girls is breast development, and the appearance of pubic hair for both sexes.

Behaviour

At this age, it is important for the child to be able to live up to situations and demands. It is important that the child's efforts receive a positive evaluation from others.

The child's wish to succeed means that she or he is more motivated to keep her attention focused on a task for a longer period of time. For instance, the child might be occupied with reaching a higher level in at computer game or getting a better grade at school.

When the child experiences mastery and that her efforts produce results, it leads to a basic sense of competence. Actions that lead to success creates a sense of mastery in the child. In the same way, however, experiencing a lack of success creates a sense of failure, incompetence, and a resulting passivity.

The child can be pre-adolescent with everything that entails. But it can also be a relatively calm period.

Social relations

The fact that the child is able to make social comparisons with others and look at him or herself from the outside has great consequences for its interaction with others.

The child becomes preoccupied with how it appears and compares to others. It takes an outside point of view of itself as well as its family. The child starts to question ways of being a family and the family she has grown up in, and she begins to compare its own family to other families with a critical eye.

Girls begin puberty about 1–2 years before boys do. On average, girls have their first period towards the end of this time.

Children at this age spend more and more time with their peers and less time with adults. It is no longer the entire group that is important. Now, close friendships and smaller groups start to develop.

It is hard to feel excluded, and the children's new mentalization skills are often used in a less than mentalizing way. It is at this stage that teen girl drama is at its highest. The hierarchy is also important to boys. It is important to not appear too girly. You must be able to handle things. There can be small manhood tests, and shared physical experiences and competition are valued.

Self

The child wants to experience itself as someone who is competent and capable of mastery which supports the development of being a me, at the same time that the child experiences itself as an active I.

The child starts to build self-confidence, where there are direct evaluations of its own worth, and feelings associated with these evaluations. The child's image of its inner life becomes increasingly nuanced.

More and more weight is put on inner qualities – which are, among other things, developed through those characteristics that the parents have used to describe the child, but also characteristics that have been emphasized by friends and teachers.

It becomes clearer that the child's understanding of itself is based on inner references. The child defines itself more mature, self-chosen sense of self through external references, such as musicians, football players, or by wearing particular brands. The child experiments with what feels like the right identity markers, so that one day he or she identifies itself with one band and one brand, while it is a completely different band and another brand that it identifies with two weeks later.

The child is increasingly able to take an outside view of itself and evaluate itself, but also to criticize itself.

Attention/cognition

The child's attention becomes focused, adjusted, and planned. The child needs this ability for challenging work at school, where it is important to be able to concentrate. At the same time, it must balance its attention with the social codes that are being exchanged during this period.

The child increasingly has to live up to higher demands at school and face more complex situations.

Not until the end of this phase, from age 11 onwards, the child develops the ability for abstract thinking which allows it to derive hypotheses and conclusions from lines of reasoning that are formulated in words. This means that the child is in fact able to make decisions based on ideas about something that is not tangible – about how something will develop, about education, about a possible relocation, etc.

How do you support development from age 9–12?

Emotions

The child is now able to talk about emotions – use it!

Enjoy the fact that your child is able to regulate emotional outbursts outside the home. Help it regulate them at home as well, if it is not yet able to do so on its own. Try saying: "I know you are really good at controlling your emotions at school, you just need to learn to do the same at home."

Physical development

Because of the increased interest in friendships, the child might start to lose interest in its extracurricular activities. As parents, it is a good idea to encourage them to persist, but also to accept that it is normal to let go of such an activity at this age.

Talk to your child about your own physical development, about the time you had your first period, or how you felt the first time you woke up after a wet dream. When you started growing pubic hair, and when you felt your body start to grow.

Make sure that you are prepared for girls' first period – show the child where it can find pads and panty liners. Let your child know that they can come to you to talk about physical development and sexuality. Parents can provide children with more certain knowledge than they can get on the internet, which is where children otherwise will typically look for information – and not necessarily on the most reliable pages.

Behaviour

The child needs to feel that its efforts have value in the eyes of others. When the child experiences that it is able to master a new skill – that its efforts pay off – it develops a fundamental sense of competence.

If the child is often unsuccessful in its efforts, lower the demands. It is important for the child's development that it experiences success and mastery.

Social relations

The child has acquired new skills which make her able to take an outside view of itself. There is plenty to learn about setting boundaries and determining which relationships are healthy and which are not. Support the child in doing this by talking to them about it in a mentalizing way.

Understand that it is important to be able to set boundaries in social relations and to test what feels good in one's relationships with others.

Accept that the child needs support to make sure that their new skillset is used constructively, so the child also treats people they do not want to be close to with respect, and so it learns how to balance being in a smaller group with being in a bigger group in a constructive way.

Recognize that the first infatuations with popstars can be a way to practice romantic love.

Avoid overstepping the child's boundaries or to lecture he or she. It is not just a matter of telling it about "the birds and the bees," but rather it is a series of talks about different topics within sexuality, big and small, which continue into puberty. Give the child age-appropriate information about online behaviour in relation to sexuality. It is advantageous that the child dares to tell its parents when she experiences something online that she does not understand.

Talk about online sexuality and porn – it is not reality, it is not what goes on in normal romantic relationships, and it is not what normal bodies look like.

By expressing sexual topics in words, you provide your child with a language for what they are experiencing, and you show them that they can always come to you.

Self

The child is starting to figure out who it is – and not just based on what its parents and others tell he or she. It tries to find out who she or he is on it own, from his or her own inner references. It is a good idea for parents to support and respect this, even though it can seem silly that the child suddenly has to show who it is through designer items, or attachment to a certain pop band, brand of clothing, or hairstyle. By supporting the child's ideas, parents show that they respect their child's choices. At the same time, it is advisable for parents to be transparent about their own attitudes.

Children at this age are particularly sensitive to negative feedback from their parents and other children. Children who are repeatedly told that they are stupid, that they destroy things, or that they are uninteresting, can internalize this and start acting accordingly.

Attention/cognition

The child broadens her span of attention when it successfully manages to regulate her attention.

It is a recurrent question why children or young people who have difficulties keeping their attention focused are able to stay very focused for long periods of time on computer games, for example. Whether or not it is a question of exercising the attention is beyond the scope of this book. However, it is entirely legal to tell the child: "You are able to do it when you play computer games. How do you think that can be translated to other situations?" This way, you recognize the child's capacity for mastery, which is always a sound basis for strengthening the child's attention and concentration.

Fill the child with knowledge when it is prepared to listen to you. It will not be long before it will not ask you anymore.

Ask open questions about the things the child sees or reads about. Explain the meaning of the word. Actively discuss what his or her book is about.

Mentalization and the 9–12-year-old child

Age	Mentalization	How do I support my child's mentalization?
9–12 years	The ability to engage in social comparison and self-evaluation is developed. The child is able to take an external view of itself and an internal view of others. The child becomes more selective about which friends it wants to hang out with. The child realizes how he or she itself, its parents, and its family structure differ from other people.	As parents, it can be a good idea to be aware that the child's recently acquired ability to mentalize means that it becomes preoccupied with differences and similarities between itself and its friends. As a consequence, it might start to voice these observations. This can seem as ill-natured drama, but in many ways learning how to mentalize resembles learning how to ride a bike – it takes practice. However, once you have learned it, you do not have to think about it. Consequently, it is always a good idea to listen to the child and discreetly guide it to take a more nuanced view of itself and other people. Help the child set boundaries in a positive way. Talk to the child about why families are different, and the advantages of other ways of life and other family structures, and the reason why other people's lives are shaped the way they are. Talk about what the child is proud of in relation to its family, its life, and its interests. Open up and take an interest in the child's emerging experiences with different lifestyles or the reason why it thinks its parents are embarrassing.

Development age 13–18

During the teenage years, the young person goes through a necessary but intense development which has impact on all six areas of development. This way, the young person trains for and tunes into adult life, where he or she has to make systemic, mentalizing, and rational decisions. Youth can be viewed as a journey made up of gradually testing boundaries and exploring the unknown in order to create a coherent sense of self. As a parent, you can sometimes feel tempted to think about this period as something to get through as quickly as possible, but as an adult you are able to influence the young person at this important stage of his or her life.

In many ways, it is a chance to support the young person in unlearning inappropriate strategies and learning new ones, since the brain at this period is in the middle of a process where some of the earlier synaptic connections disappear and others become stronger and more specialized. When, as a parent, you become frustrated with your teenager, you must remember that its behaviour reflects that positive forces are at work such as looking for new social engagements, new friendships, heightened vitality, and creative exploration (Siegel 2013).

During the teenage years, large parts of the brain are developing and being rebuilt (Fonagy et al. 2007) – especially those parts of the brain that deal with taking perspective, rational decision making, and mentalization. Because of this rebuilding, the more instinctive and emotional parts of the brain are in control rather than the thinking and rational parts. This is why young people are able to express intense emotions and have difficulties regulating them. They can switch between being extremely good and really lousy at understanding other people's emotions. This also explains the heightened impulsivity and sensation-seeking behaviour. The extent to which they experience drama and intense emotions is a complex interaction between genetics and environment, and not all young people experience this period as tumultuous and dramatic.

Suggestions and strategies

Do your best to maintain your ability to mentalize. Talk to others who can help you stay mentalizing. Try to remember the intensity of your own emotions as a young person – a hotchpotch of loneliness, being in love, confusion, insecurity, and happiness.

Example

15-year-old Nancy thinks her parents are completely unfair for not allowing her to go to a big music festival. She asks both her mother and her father, gives arguments, gets angry, and calls them idiots who want to keep her locked up like Rapunzel, alone in her tower. Finally, she texts her mother: "It makes me really sad and I feel empty inside when my own mother doesn't listen to me. You have to give me space to grow up and be with my friends, because you know my friends mean *everything* to me. That's why I'll do anything not to feel excluded. I honestly can't see what the problem is – it isn't dangerous to go to a concert."

MODEL DEVELOPMENT AGE 13–18

Figure 3.4

Emotions

During the teenage years, the young person is able to put their emotions into context and to understand complex emotions in itself and in others. The ability to regulate emotions improves but is challenged by its new ability to think in the abstract. The world becomes more complex and confusing. That is why, as a parent, you experience such a confusing mixture of a young person who is sometimes mature, well-reflected, and understanding of its own and others' emotions, and at other times she cannot bear the complexity of the world and reacts as a small, immature child when it comes to handling its emotions: "Why do they keep having children in Africa when there is famine? They should just stop."

Young people's emotions can be changeable and unpredictable, and they are hypersensitive towards them. Young people not only experience the intense emotions, they also often stage these emotions themselves. This can involve emotions at both ends of the spectrum, from anger and jealousy to indifference.

The young people must break free from their parents, and that is a difficult process. For some, the process is associated with intense emotions – love for the parents can quickly change into outright dislike.

Behaviour

During the teenage years, your child's behaviour often seems badly regulated. Because it now has the ability to mentalize, the world appears more complex and sometimes overwhelming. In order to take in all this complexity, the young person will often turn from complexity to simplicity. This is evident in its behaviour, such as mindless internet surfing, playing computer games featuring good and evil, or searching for simplicity in reality shows or romantic stories where emotions are presented as simple and intense.

Put in popular terms, the brain is bored during the teenage years. Risk-taking behaviour generates a kind of reward because neurotransmitters such as adrenaline and dopamine are released in the brain. This is one of the reasons why there is more risk-taking behaviour during this time. This can be manifested in different ways, such as playing conjuring games, shoplifting, playing drinking games, experimenting with drugs, sexual behaviour, petty crime, dangerous games such as climbing on to a train, or destructive online behaviour where you send and share inappropriate images and comments.

Research shows that young people's risk-taking behaviour grows in proportion to the number of people that are together – the more young people in the same room, the more risk-taking behaviour.

Physical development

This period involves massive physical changes. Firstly, the size of the body changes radically. The young person reaches sexual maturity and grows rapidly during this developmental phase. Suddenly, the world, which used to be relatively neutral, is painted in all the colours of sexuality.

It is a challenge to settle into one's new body, and many young people are unhappy with their bodies. Social media, and the body ideals presented at such platforms, may contribute to the fact that more and more teenagers develop a negative body image.

Due to hormonal changes, young people are increasingly sexually curious, and most of them make their sexual debut during this time.

The first sexual experiences can be challenged by the fact that today, the internet has given many young people unrealistic ideas about sex. If the information from the internet is considered as the norm, it can easily result lead to performance anxiety and feelings of inferiority.

The hormonal changes also influence the teenager's circadian rhythm. Teenagers need more sleep and they often sleep irregularly, going to bed late and getting up late.

Self

Young people start to develop an inner life that the adults is not a part of, such as crushes and knowledge about their friends' inner lives.

Identity is the dominant theme of this period and the young person experiments with who it is by expressing itself through the music, attitudes, and clothes etc. that they choose – and do not choose.

The young person becomes more self-aware and self-reflective. A more

Social relations

At this age, young people spend much more time with their peers than with adults. It is a natural part of the independence process to change from being dependent on adults, to being dependent peers, before finally becoming independent.

Young people are extremely sensitive to being excluded from the group. It is very important to fit in and young people will often abandon the truth, their own values, and the trust of their family and friends, in favour of being part of the group.

To their mind, interaction that stimulates development usually only happens in friendships. Friends mean everything, but it is actually very important for young people's positive development that their parents are involved and have the ability to set boundaries as well as being supportive and mentalizing.

It can be hard to bear the child's process of liberation because it fluctuates between distance and closeness: "I can do everything on my own, so leave me alone!" vs. "Why are you never there for me?"

When breaking away from one's first social relations – one's parents – it is normal to focus on difference, embarrassment, and thereby criticism and distancing oneself.

Attention and cognition

Teenagers' ability to structure, plan, and take a comprehensive view of things is improved. They are also able to understand concepts and abstract ideas in a way that they have not been able to up until now. Their improved cognitive complexity means that the young person must integrate a range of highly complex ideas about its own and others' emotions and motivation.

It is confusing for parents that the young person on the one hand stable and coherent sense of self is developed that is not dependent on parents and friends: "I am smart. I am a good person. I am someone who likes to dance. I am someone who is never the first choice" and so on. The essence of this sense of "who I am" is consolidated during late adolescence. During the teenage years, the young person starts to perceive itself as a unity that persists over time: "I am basically the same person today that I was yesterday."

During late adolescence, some young people need some time to think where they consolidate the self by examining all those changes they have undergone during their teenage years.

is developing and improving its cognitive skills, while on the other hand situations arise where its judgment and decision-making abilities seem challenged, given that it can partake in dangerous activities despite the fact that it ought to be able to consider the possible negative consequences.

The teenage brain follows the rule of "use it" or "lose it." This means that those abilities that are not exercised will more or less disappear, while those abilities that *are* exercised will develop and become more specialized.

How do you support development from age 13–18?

Emotions

All the strategies that you have had to use as a parent to support the child's emotional development should be applied during this period – but with respect and care for a young person who is beginning to distance itself from its parents.

If the teenager is inaccessible and ill-tempered at home, it is important to pay attention to whether it is under pressure in other areas of her life. That does not excuse her behaviour, but it makes it easier to handle the situation in a mentalizing way.

Do not underestimate the importance of your own emotions. It can be very emotionally taxing to be a part of the young person's mood swings, unpredictability, and risk-taking. It does not make things easier if the young person directs its frustrations and negative emotions towards you.

Behaviour

Teenagers need boundaries, but mentalizing boundaries. There needs to be a balance between rigidity and chaos (see p. 76). It can be a good idea to establish a set of ground rules, such as the time you expect your teenager to be back home in the evenings, how you talk to each other, how much alcohol it is allowed to drink, and which household chores it is responsible for.

When setting such boundaries, it can be a good idea to remember that starting a sentence with: "Don't . . ." can easily have the opposite effect, as an encouragement. It is better to formulate a sentence such as: "It is good that you do not leave you friends behind at a party – good friends take care of each other, and they leave together."

If your child engages in risk-taking behaviour, find other ways to satisfy this need for excitement than through danger. For example, if your teenager likes cars and speed, take it to a go-kart track with its friends.

Physical development

Radical bodily changes are challenging for a teenager. They happen at the same time that the young person no longer seeks support from its parents to the same extent.

This can be a tricky balancing act. One the one hand, young people really need everything that is going on with their body to be

Social relations

The young person feels safe when they experience the adult as a lighthouse that is stable and always available. Young people sail in and out of the home, but sometimes they need you to be there: Regulated, accountable and mentalizing.

During this period, young people's relations to others have a great normalized: periods, masturbation, premature ejaculation, pimples, hair growth, developing body parts, and not least budding sexuality. On the other hand, they cannot bear that their parents meddle in relation to their "new" body.

Try to remember how you felt during that period yourself, and then gently try to be the young person's supportive lighthouse, which is both mentalizing, offers knowledge, and respects his or her personal boundaries.

Accept it if the young person chooses to talk to other adults about these things. It might be stepparents, a soccer coach, a teacher, or a friend's parents. It can feel like a loss not to be her first choice anymore, but it is a natural part of development.

impact on their development. Support the young person in experiencing different social relations, even if they are not the ones you would have chosen. Be supportive of the teenager's relationships. Offer to host parties or to drive them to and from social events. Take it seriously if the young person feels bullied or isolated.

The first love can be very intense, and so can the first break-up. Teenagers do not have the adult's experience that you are able to love again. Friendships that fall apart can also be felt intensely.

The rejections can take their toll on even the strongest parent. Remember that natural forces are at work!

When you have experienced a strong bond with another person, it can require a lot of energy to break free and establish a new, mature "adult-to-adult"-relation between parents and child. In order to endure this process, it can be a good idea to use your personal network to vent and to normalize yourself, so you can continue to be a role model for your child when it comes to handling social relations – even when another storm comes along.

Self

The best way for parents to support the child's development of self is by being Open, Balanced, Empathic, Curious, and Patient in relation to the adult that your teenager is in the process of becoming – even when it tries out sides of itself that differ from the way its parents perceive him or her.

It can offend the parents' values when their child is either withdrawn or outgoing, experiments with sexuality, or hang out with friends that they do not approve of.

When it is difficult to see the young person's positive sides, it can be helpful to appreciate that the young person's sometimes inappropriate behaviour also reflects creativity and a passion for life.

Attention and cognition

At this age, parents can gently and respectfully guide the child's attention in certain directions. In doing this, you also support cognitive development.

When helping your child with its homework, do it in a respectful way. Remember to be Regulated, Accountable, and Mentalizing. Ensure that the young person experiences a sense of success. Teenagers need to feel important and independent.

When you assist the child with her homework, the task at hand must be as manageable as possible. If the child has fallen behind in several subjects, break it down into something manageable: "Let's spend 20 minutes on equations."

Help your teenager recognize its own resources or strengths by being aware of them yourself. For example, write down your teenager's resources when you feel that you are losing sight of them.

If the young person is going through a time where they seem withdrawn and in need of a break, it is important to pay special attention, because many mental illnesses develop during the teenage years – but at the same time, it is completely normal to need a break sometimes to consolidate the self.

Help it understand the importance of paying attention in school. But remember that the young person is more than its attention and cognition. Create a balance and acknowledge all the different aspects of the young person.

Most teenagers are afraid of being outsiders, which can motivate them to do well.

Pay attention to what the young person says about motivation itself and repeat it: "You said that you wanted to study more because you want to do well on the midterm."

Mentalization and the 13–18-year-old teenager

Age	Mentalization	How do I support my child's mentalization?
13–18 years	The young person's ability for mentalization is developed and improved throughout its teenage years. The young person refines its understanding of herself and others and its language for mental states is similarly boosted. If you view the child as a ship on the ocean, the small child is only able to see itself, the lighthouse, and another ship. During the teenage years, a quantum leap happens, so that the young person is now able to see the light from all the ships, but the challenge is that it is easily overwhelmed by the complexity. This can be a contributing factor to the young person's many fluctuations and mentalization failures. Since the ability is still new to them, young people spend a lot more energy on mentalization than adults do. More abstract ideas about mental states can put such a considerable	Parents' ability to mentalize in relation to their teenager is important for the teenager's continuous development of mentalization. The ability to mentalize develops throughout one's life, and even though it can sometimes appear fully developed the ability is shifty, and therefore you cannot expect the same from young people that you can from adults in terms of mentalization. At this stage, the young person is in need of adults who are sympathetic and patient towards it developing mentalization ability. It is also important that the adults are transparent about their own mental states – even when they get angry or scared. That way, parents help the young person understand others and become role models for mastering one's mental states in a different way than through physical action or bodily symptoms (such as headache, stomach ache). How the young person handles the challenges that arise as a consequence of their newly acquired mentalizing and cognitive skills depend not only on the mental structures of the individual teenager, but also on

Age	Mentalization	How do I support my child's mentalization?
	mental load on the young person that it leads to breakdown of mentalization and a tendency to social withdrawal, thereby running the risk of increasingly acting out conflicts. The young person's mental image of its parents also changes. It becomes more critical, but at the same time more nuanced and realistic. The image of the fantastic dad who can do anything is destroyed in favour of a more nuanced image.	the degree to which the parents and the surroundings are able to support the teenager in those situations where its ability to mentalize is weakened. It is crucial that you relate to the young person as an independent individual who is alternating between extremes of excessive intimacy and distance. Even though it can be hard, you must also be able to endure the less than idealized image of yourself that the young person is in the process of developing. Inflicting shame on and distancing oneself from the young person can even undermine its psychological self.

Development promoting interaction – obtaining skills

Children must be met with challenges and demands that are appropriate for their developmental age. If you do not comply with this, it is equivalent to presenting a preschooler with a high school curriculum, in which case the child as well as the parents can easily come to feel flawed and unsuccessful.

Some children have special challenges or have experienced things in their life which means that they have spent their energy on something other than development during a period of their lives. However, in addition to this, children can be at different stages of development at different times. When the one-year-old is tired, it is less able to regulate its emotions than when it is well-rested. When the teenager is in the musical at school, its social skills express themselves more than when it is at home, where it must interact with her mother in an appropriate way. You could describe the child as a developing moving target (Perry & Szalavitz 2011).

As parents, you must adjust the challenges to the individual child's developmental level in relation to the areas: emotions, behaviour, social relations, self, and attention/cognition. If you feel that your child is not developing in a positive direction, you should figure out how to adjust your expectations by talking about the child's current developmental level as opposed to its chronological age, that is, is the date on the child's birth certificate.

Suggestions and strategies

If you, as parents, accidentally set expectations for your child that are too high for their developmental level, the child is unable to make use of the development promoting interaction offered by its parents.

Example

Ella was born with a heart defect. Her first year of life was marked by several potentially fatal operations which inflicted anxiety, chaos, and worry on her parents. Ella spent all her energy on surviving, as did her parents. Fortunately, things ended well. At age 5, Ella was given a clean bill of health.

However, because of her illness, Ella has not had a chance at the development promoting interaction that she needed. It is hard for her kindergarten teachers to understand Ella's level of immaturity, since her parents have taught their daughter to behave in a way that is suitable for her age. She has good table manners and is aware of age-appropriate norms of social behaviour, but the moment she has to play with other children, she is like a baby. She does not understand the concept of taking turns, she will not share, and she is unable to express her emotions and will kick and hit if she feels that she has been treated unfairly.

It helps the staff when they understand that, when it comes to social relations, emotions, and mentalization, Ella is at a basic level and she should be approached as a small child even though she is at the age-appropriate level in other areas.

Model obtaining skills

Write down the child's developmental age alongside its actual age in relation to the six areas. The model is intended as an instrument for reflection, not as a measurement of development.

Emotions

Being able to register, categorize, verbalize, and regulate emotions and to understand that emotions are complex. The ability to recognize emotions in others.

Behaviour

Age-appropriate behaviour such as having table manners, knowing how to greet others, knowing how to behave outside of the home, and being able to sit still.

Physical development

Being able to feel cold and warm, having age-appropriate motor skills, being able to feel hungry and full, to feel tired, and the ability to physically create a sense of calm within one's body.

Relationships

Having close and positive relationships with others, including one's parents, friends, pets, neighbours, family members, or others. Being able to enter into equal relationships with peers. Having age-appropriate social skills such as understanding the concept of taking turns and being a part of social hierarchies.

Sense of self

Having a coherent sense of "me" – with high self-esteem as a result of positive mirroring. Experiencing a sense of a positive, acting "I" – self-confidence and believing that you can affect the world in a positive way and that you can succeed in reaching your goal, which involves having a sense that your actions and behaviour is recognized and leads to the desired objectives.

Attention/cognition

Having an age-appropriate ability to focus one's attention and concentrate in different contexts. Having an age-appropriate level of cognitive functioning. Paying attention in class, knowing common facts such as: who is the president, etc.

Mentalization

The ability to understand themselves and others based on underlying mental states.

Children aged 0–3 should be met with mentalization. They only have the seed of mentalization themselves.

Children aged 4–8 are at the early stages of mentalization.

9–12-year-olds develop the ability to make social comparisons which leads them to use and abuse the ability to evaluate themselves and others.

13–18-year-olds continuously develop their ability to mentalize to more advanced levels, but they experience many mentalization failures.

Chapter 4

The mentalization toolbox

In Chapter 3, we suggested ways in which parents can support their child's development. In this part, we examine two areas of development in depth, namely behaviour and emotions. Parents are often more focused on regulating the child's behaviour, but the other area is equally important for the child, as one must have an understanding of one's emotions in order to be able to mentalize, make personal choices, cooperate, and adapt to changing circumstances.

The mentalization toolbox provides you with specific tools for raising children and makes suggestions about the best ways to encourage good behaviour while also supporting emotional development. As we shall see, the development of these two areas are inseparably linked.

The development of good or appropriate behaviour is of great importance to parents as well as children, since it is an integral part of creating an environment in which everyone can thrive. When it comes to behaviour, it is important to appreciate what the child has yet to develop while also considering whether the undesirable behaviour might owe to a lack of abilities in another area, in which case the desired behaviour cannot be learned until the other abilities have been acquired. For instance, a temper tantrum can seldom be abated unless you also practice emotional self-regulation with the child.

All in all, the ability to recognize and understand your own and others' emotions and to regulate them is a huge advantage for learning to behave in a way that creates a good environment. You need to set a course for your behaviour and use your emotions as a compass so that they can help you find your way in the world. To this end, Chapter 4 concludes with a number of models that illustrate how you best support your child's emotional development. Put more simply: "Emotions are the royal road to mentalization." The specific models relate to the development of children's abilities to register, categorize, verbalize, and regulate emotions. Children require parents who agree on the importance of emotions in order to gain an optimum understanding of their own emotions – that is, parents who have an emotional awareness and who also recognize negative emotions as an opportunity to teach their child something important (Gottman 1999).

The toolbox

The toolbox illustrates the best way to regulate children's behaviour. It is based on knowledge about the brain and how children learn new behaviour. Simply put, the right side of the brain is creative, emotional, and image-creating, while the left side is logical, linguistic, and rational (Siegel 2012). Children require both sides of their brain equally in order to become a well-rounded, well-functioning person. Parents who are aware of this have a unique opportunity to create learning situations that can help children integrate the two sides of their brain.

Suggestions and strategies

You should be aware that what might appear to be bad behaviour is often just a reflection of the fact that the child has not yet learned to regulate other areas of development, such as emotions. Also, take care to consider that spending quality time together at home is not a question of tools and toolboxes but rather is about focusing on personal interaction. The toolbox is just a metaphor used to illustrate the layers of tools for you to keep in mind when you face a challenge in relation to your child.

Example

Four-year-old Louis' cousin Oscar, who is 2 years old, has come to stay with him for a few days. When Oscar wakes up the next morning, he is upset and misses his mother. Louis' mother comforts Oscar and gets out a game for them that has a lot of toy fish. When Louis' mother leaves them for a short while, Louis takes all the fish from the game. Oscar says: "Mustn't" and starts to cry again. Louis' mom thinks: "Perhaps Louis is jealous because he thinks Oscar gets too much attention. I'd like to teach him to be nice to younger children." She regulates herself and then the children. Then she puts her arms around Louis and says: "I understand that you don't like it when mom is so focused on Oscar (right side) but he is just a little boy and not as big as you, and he misses his mother, so he would like to play with the fish for the game (left side)." Louis returns the fish to the game and the mother thinks: "I didn't need to reach the bottom of the toolbox in this situation."

MODEL **THE TOOLBOX**

Figure 4.1

The toolbox consists of:

- Reflections before opening the box.
- Regulating yourself first.
- Regulating the child.
- Right side of the box – support and lubricate.
- Left side of the box – setting the course.
- The bottom of the toolbox – the part that should be used the least.

Reflections before opening the box

We recommend that you consider the best way to create a learning environment for your child before you open the toolbox. Behaviour regulation is about teaching the child something it has not yet been able to do. When parents see their child behaving badly, it can be helpful to look at it the following way: "What is it the child has not yet learned that makes him/her react this way?" And tell the child: "This is something you haven't learned yet, but you will eventually."

Parents should also be aware that it is easier to teach their child to behave a certain way if the child experiences the behaviour as meaningful. In order to support the child's learning, parents must be mentalizing towards the child and express an interest in understanding its behaviour. They must also be aware of the child's current developmental level. Children are born to learn, so when you get it right the child will often enjoy learning. When you have to learn something, it is good to be prepared. This applies to great and small matters: "Five more minutes, then you must turn off your iPad," or "As of Monday, you must cycle to school on your own."

Repetition and routines are essential when it comes to learning. When you repeat something, you get better. Routines give you a sense that "that is how we do it in this family," such as when it is time for bed, the rituals connected with bedtime, or table manners. It is important that they are not too rigid but rather adapted to the child's development and family life. Without routines, everyday life becomes chaotic, with negative consequences for everyone.

Suggestions and strategies

When you want your child to learn something, make it a priority. Signal to the child when there is something important to learn by walking over to the child and directing your own as well as the child's attention towards the thing that needs to be learned.

Example

Nine-year-old Amanda suffered from a sore throat at the beginning of her summer vacation and has been sleeping in her parents' bed for comfort. However, now school has started again. Amanda's parents want her to sleep in her own bed again. They explain to Amanda that she is about to learn something she has not been able to do yet. They tell her that everyone sleeps better when there are not so many people in the bed. They agree on a time where Amanda will go back to sleeping in her own bed and ask her if there is anything that makes her anxious about it. Everything runs surprisingly smoothly. The father tucks Amanda in, since he is best at keeping things simple, and after this Amanda sleeps in her own bed.

MODEL REFLECTIONS BEFORE OPENING THE BOX

Figure 4.2

How do you do it?

- Mentalize.
- Ask yourself:
    - What does the child need to learn?
    - Does the task make sense to the child?
    - Has the child reached the right developmental level to master the challenge?
- Prepare.
- Repeat (rules and routines).
- Prioritize the thing that needs to be learned.

Regulating yourself first – stay calm

Learning to regulate yourself can be a lifelong challenge. It might seem inadvisable to spend time on self-regulation that takes up time as well as energy, but if the adult is well-regulated and emotionally well-balanced, conflicts can be avoided and there is a greater opportunity for learning.

When things reach a critical point, it can be a good idea to mentalize yourself – to be aware of your own emotions, needs, and goals – but it is not necessarily a good idea to mentalize your child because you risk hanging on to a negative conception of what goes on in the child's mind: "He is just out to ruin everything for me," "he is just like his father," or "she uses me."

Different things can support self-regulation depending on the person and the situation, but during times of peace, explain to your child why you act the way you do: "When mom is upset, I go to the kitchen to be alone. I do not mean to abandon you, but it helps me calm myself down." That way, your child learns that sometimes adults also need strategies for handling intense emotions.

Suggestions and strategies

Pay attention to which strategies help you regulate yourself. It might be something entirely different from what we have suggested here. Write it down and practice various techniques until you find your own personal strategy.

Example

A father has just picked up his two sons from after-school care and is heading home after a long day. Eight-year-old Ollie suddenly refuses to walk any further. He lays down on the pavement and stays put. Two-year-old Jake, who is sitting in his stroller, complains that he is cold. One of the shopping bags is about to fall out from under the stroller, and the father is carrying another one, its plastic handle fighting against gravity. The father can feel that he is getting angry. He feels like kicking Ollie, who is sprawling on the ground in his snowsuit.

He reminds himself that he needs to regulate himself using his favourite technique, which involves his working memory. It usually works, and he looks around in the twilight and wonders how many privet hedges he can see from this position and "if you multiplied that with the number of houses, how much would that add up to?" Slowly, he feels himself calm down and his breathing changes and becomes more even. He looks at the situation from the outside – and uses the toolbox.

MODEL REGULATING YOURSELF FIRST

How do you do it?

Use your "helpful thoughts": "I can handle this," "I am a good parent," "If I am calm, it calms my child."

Use your working memory: "Counting backwards from 10," "Saying 10 words in English" (Elvén & Wiman 2016).

Use movements – consciously making yourself smile sends positive signals to the brain (Siegel & Bryson 2012). Jumping or walking can release anger from the body. Encourage the child to join you: "Let's take a walk around the house and talk about it."

Take a break – walk away – drink a glass of water, or listen to your own breathing.

Drink water.

Go out of doors and enjoy nature.

Talk to another mentalizing adult.

Use your own strategies.

Figure 4.3

Regulating the child

In order to be open to learning, the adult and the child both need to be regulated and within their window of tolerance. When the child's emotions are at their most intense, the best line of action is to distract the child's attention. This is one of the oldest tricks in the book which all parents know, for example when you are at the supermarket and your 3-year-old throws himself on the floor and yells: "I want a lollipop!" and you reply: "Look at the cute teddy bear over there." Humour can also be a strategy for regulating the child's emotions. When we laugh together, we move around the emotional compass.

In terms of mirror neurons (see the introduction), if adult and child make eye contact when experiencing intense emotions, they will regulate each other upwards in emotional intensity. Keeping eye contact can be experienced as a power struggle or continued negotiation – so, when dealing with intense emotions, you should avoid eye contact or place yourself below eye level. Sit down on the bed or on the floor and use your body language to communicate reassurance and support and that you do not want conflict and fight. On the next page you will find a model with more suggestions for emotion regulation.

Suggestions and strategies

During times of peace, you can talk to your child about the best way to provide support when it experiences intense emotions.

Example

On a summer afternoon, 6-year-old Victor is relaxing in the sun with his mother and her friend. Victor has been playing in the sandbox, but now he hears the sound of the ice cream truck and yells: "I want ice cream!" Victor has difficulty regulating his emotions on his own and his mother thinks to herself: "What Victor needs to learn right now is that you don't always get what you want." Even though she would rather have continued chatting with her friend, she turns her attention to Victor and says: "I know that hearing the sound of the truck makes you want an ice cream, but you have already had cake today, so it won't do." She crouches down in front of Victor to bring them at the same eye level, and gently puts her hand on his arm. Victor shakes her hand off and slaps it, takes the napkin from his mother's friend's plate and tosses it on the ground as he yells: "I want ice cream, ice cream, ice cream!" His mother says: "Hey, what were you building in the sandbox? I bet I can get over there before you to see!" Victor rushes to the sandbox and his mother follows him. Fortunately, the ice cream truck does not ring its bell during the next few minutes.

MODEL **REGULATING THE CHILD**

Use distraction.

Use humour – do not laugh at the child, but with it.

Avoid eye contact – it intensifies emotions.

Go below eye level – it regulates emotions.

Surprise the child positively – let the child gain new and positive experiences with conflict resolutions, for instance: "I'm going to bake a cake, would you like to help me whip the cream?"

Make yourself seem a little useless, as it supports mentalization, for example: "Wow, even you father couldn't carry such a heavy plate!"

Breathe – if you are dealing with a small child, you can sit beside it and place your hand gently on its tummy while saying: "Take a deep breath." At the same time, show the child how to do it.

Compete – for some children (especially little boys), it can be a good idea to start a competition, such as: "Who can get their jacket on the fastest?" or "I'll race you to the top of the hill!"

Figure 4.4

The right side of the toolbox – support and lubricate

When you are about to teach the child a new behaviour, you begin by using the right side of the toolbox. This side corresponds to the right side of the brain which is responsible for emotions, mentalization, and creativity. In the toolbox, this is where you find the softer tools such as the cleaning rag and lubricant. This means that you should approach your child gently and calmly, listen to and support it, acknowledge its feelings, and make active use of mirror neurons by behaving the way you want your child to behave. Using mirror neurons can be seen as a kind of training wheel for the behaviour you want your child to learn. Furthermore, it is important that you show your child that you trust it.

Suggestions and strategies

It is particularly important to use the right side of the brain to acknowledge the small child (age 0–3), since the child is not yet able to comprehend logic and responsibility at this age. However, if you keep to this side of the toolbox in relation to older children, it does not encourage development – at least only to a limited extent.

Example

Normally, 8-year-old Laura spends 20 minutes every day reading, but today she refuses. Her mother sits down next to her and softly says: "You usually like to read. Why don't you want to read today?" She puts her hand gently on Laura's knee and then keeps quiet. Laura says that since the sun is shining, she wants to go outside and play with the sprinkler, and that she loves to jump on the trampoline and play with the sprinkler. Her mother says: "I understand that you want to do that and I am so proud that you are able to explain it to me so that I can understand you better, but you are actually really good at reading and you have gotten so good at doing it every day. Do you want to continue with the book we have already started reading, or would you rather read something in your magazine?" Laura's mother picks up a book herself and starts to read. After a short while, Laura starts to read as well. Afterwards, her mother praises her: "You did it even though you didn't feel like it to begin with. You persisted, even when it was hard. That was really well done."

MODEL **RIGHT SIDE OF THE TOOLBOX**

Lubri-
cant

Support
and
lubricate

Figure 4.5

How do you do it?

- Use non-verbal signals, for example a soft, considerate tone of voice (Csibra 2010).
- Positive physical touch, for example a hand gently stroking the child's back or softly touching its shoulder (for more on the importance of hugs, see p. 203). Touch is effective, but the child needs to be regulated first. Otherwise, the child may experience it as a threat. Similarly, in the case of teenagers, it might have a provoking rather than a calming effect.
- Use words to acknowledge emotions: "I understand why it made you so angry that you hit him," or "I understand that you are so excited about the party that you think midnight is too early for me to pick you up" (remember the gangway, p. 64).
- Listen and support. Before crossing the gangway to the child, you must listen to it to try to understand what is going on and take it seriously. You might feel tempted to explain and talk away, but you should begin by listening and asking short questions instead: "Help me understand. Why did you hit him?" or "Why don't you want to wear your shoes?"
- Show that you have trust in the child by saying: "I know it is hard, but I am sure you can do it if you try a little bit harder."
- Make active use of mirror neurons by doing the things you want to teach your child to do. For example, if you want your child to go out the door, you can go to the door yourself and open it. When you want the child to tidy up, you can begin doing so without finishing.

The left side of the toolbox – setting the course

When we open the left side of the toolbox, we address the logical, linguistic part of the brain – the one that is able to learn something new. Parents are usually in a hurry to get to this part, to verbalize the unwanted behaviour, and to teach the child something new. However, it is much more productive to wait until the child is ready. The left side of the brain contains tools that set the course for the behaviour you want to teach your child. Countless research experiments have shown that children feel more secure when their parents stand their ground and behave reliably. It is reassuring for children when they know what to expect from their parents. Research also shows that there are fewer conflicts in families where children experience clear boundaries (Siegel 2013; Forster 2014).

Suggestions and strategies

It might be a good idea to examine whether the strategies you use as a parent are influenced by your own personal experiences and then to actively reflect on and consider whether you want to raise your own children in the same way. Another good tip is to avoid talking too much – stick to what is most important. Parents tend to make long speeches during which the child stops listening – and therefore does not learn anything. As a rule of thumb, a few well-chosen words are more effective (Siegel & Bryson 2014).

Example

A 3-year-old girl is jumping on the bed at her grandmother's house. Her father says: "Five more jumps, then we are leaving." When the girl has jumped five times, the father says: "Time to go," but the girl yells: "I want to keep jumping!" Her father replies: "I understand that, since it is so much fun to jump in grandma's bed, but it is really time to go home now." He keeps his voice calm, and gently picks his daughter up from the bed: "Those were some really impressive jumps you did, maybe you can do it again the next time we visit grandma."

MODEL **LEFT SIDE OF THE TOOLBOX**

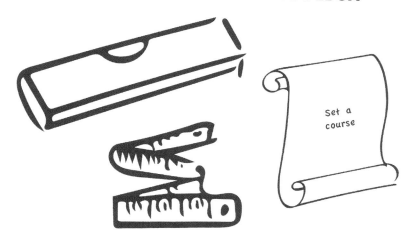

Set a course

Figure 4.6

How do you do it?

- Address the child in a positive way when making demands.
- Only set one task at a time – little children cannot contain more than one message in their memory at a time, and even older children give up if they feel overwhelmed.
- Involve the child and make it attractive for it to live up to your demands. It is true for both children and adults that when you feel involved, you feel more respected, and therefore you are more likely to cooperate.
- If you see others exhibiting the behaviour, praise them.
- Praise the children for what they are doing and remember to encourage the desired behaviour (see p. 14 for information about process praise).
- Give options: "You have to put on clothes now, but it is up to you whether you want to wear the red or the green shirt." This makes the child feel acknowledged and respected.
- Ignore undesirable behaviour – shift your attention away from the child – move your attention back to the child when it displays the desired behaviour.
- Hold on to your demands in a mentalizing way. Sometimes, there are good reasons not to do this, but in general it is important that children experience clear boundaries that are not easily changed.

The bottom of the toolbox

When the child's behaviour is highly inappropriate, it can be necessary to dig through to the bottom of the toolbox for the heavy tools. The heaviest tool is the relationship, so if the child continues to exhibit bad behaviour over an extended period of time, it can be a good idea that the adults that are close to the child sit down together to talk about the child's needs. The child can also participate in such meetings.

There are two central points regarding the bottom of the toolbox. Firstly, you must attempt to use all the other tools first. For some children, sitting down for a serious conversation with their parents is the worst thing imaginable, because then you are really in trouble. You should consider beforehand how to make the meeting mentalizing and emphasize the importance of identifying the underlying reasons for the behaviour.

Secondly, you can make use of natural consequences immediately following the child's behaviour: "If you forgot your gym clothes, you will just have to go back and get them yourself." Sometimes, we need to see that things have real consequences. Older children are more likely to learn from these kinds of consequences.

Suggestions and strategies

After a conflict, it is important to re-establish the relationship – and this is the adult's responsibility. It is a great opportunity for children to learn that you even though might disagree and have conflicts, you will find one another again afterwards and re-establish the connection.

Example

Sixteen-year-old Emily is on holiday in Paris with her parents and her younger brother. From the beginning, Emily has a very negative attitude. Everything is stupid, and often she does not even care to answer when she is spoken to. Emily's brother tells their mother: "If this continues, I'll become really upset, because she'll ruin my vacation." In the morning, Emily's mother suggests that she and Emily pick up breakfast together. As they are walking, she says to Emily: "You can't behave that way on our family vacation. What's wrong?" Emily tells her that she just feels grumpy. Emily's mother replies: "I really understand that it's difficult to feel that way, but you´ll just have to hide as best you can, otherwise you'll ruin the holiday for the rest of us. If your mood continues like this, you'll just have to spend the day alone because we don't want you to spoil our holiday." Emily pulls herself together and for the rest of the holiday she is much more willing to cooperate. When they return home, however, she is back to being moody – but then again, she is just a teenager.

MODEL THE BOTTOM OF THE TOOLBOX

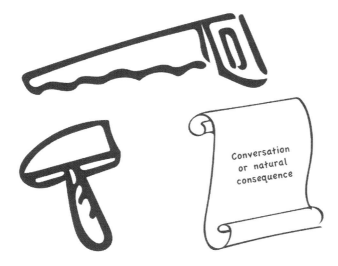

Figure 4.7

How do you do it?

- The adults around the child sit down and talk – depending on the age, the child can participate too. This is also known as the reflect and repair meeting (see the Reflect and Repair questionnaire on page 142).
- Use natural consequences – simple and relevant – natural and not punitive. As far as possible, they should be instant, that is they should occur the same day as the incident they are supposed to regulate. It is bad for a child to wake up to a new day and then experience a consequence from something that happened the day before. In some cases, for instance if a teenager has thrown a party that has gotten out of control, it makes sense that he or she is not allowed to throw another party for a while.
- After a conflict, the relationship must be re-established.

Reflect and repair

Following a mentalization breakdown that has led to particularly bad behaviour, parents and child can take time to reflect on what happened. You should not hold a reflect and repair meeting until emotions have cooled down and everyone has re-established their ability to mentalize. Together, you sit down and talk about what happened. You can look at what happened immediately prior to the burst of anger and talk about the underlying reasons for the behaviour.

The purpose of such as meeting can be to determine how to repair what has happened. You should encourage the young person to make suggestions about how this can be done (Rossouw 2012). Sometimes, this means that you determine the appropriate consequences, such as deciding whether they should apologize to someone who got scared or, if something was broken, whether they should pay for it with their pocket money. This gives the child and the carers an opportunity to understand and make sense of the behaviour. This way, consequences and repairing aftermath take place within a mentalizing framework. Reflect and repair meetings are meant for older children, and teenagers in particular.

Suggestions and strategies

You do not have to stick rigidly to the Reflect and Repair questionnaire, but you can use it as a way to begin conversations about understanding and repairing following a particularly bad episode. If the child is okay with it, you can keep the reflect and repair form and bring it out again to learn from episodes that have been very hard.

Example

The parents of 13-year-old Toby are contacted because he and two friends have been caught putting bangers in a mailbox and blowing it up. At the reflect and repair meeting, it turns out that Toby finds it hard to say no to his friends and that he thinks that everything involving blasting powder is really fascinating. He explains that he actually suggested that they find something else to blow up, but that he felt a rush through his body when the mailbox blew up.

Toby tells them that he thinks that the reason why the man who has contacted his parents is so angry is that he was actually in Afghanistan, and as they discuss it, Toby gets really embarrassed. They agree that they will contact the parents of the other two boys and that the boys should go together to apologize to the man. They agree that the boys should make payments until the mailbox is payed for. Finally, they discuss another way for Toby to feel the rush that young people are easily drawn to. They agree to go to a go-kart racing track once the mailbox has been paid for.

MODEL **REFLECT AND REPAIR**

How did you experience what happened? – Explain what you thought and
what you felt.

_____

_____

_____

How do you think others experienced the situation?

_____

_____

_____

What can you do to make amends for what happened (apologize, pay compensation etc.)?

_____

_____

_____

_____

Figure 4.8

The emotional compass

Basic emotions are emotions that are present even in newborn children. We are born with them, but the child is unable to use its innate compass to navigate unless it enters into an interaction that encourages development, through which the child learns to register, categorize, and verbalize emotions. This happens when the adult recognizes an emotion in the child, mirrors the emotions, and puts it into words. When the child is older, the adult can talk about emotions that she has experienced herself: "When I was young, one of my friends kissed my boyfriend, which made me jealous and really angry." It is important to create an environment in which the child feels that it is safe to talk about emotions. The ability to express one's emotions is developed within a close and secure relationship with a carer. It can be both impractical and disadvantageous to tell everyone everything about one's emotional states. Along the road, the child learns how to dial its emotions either up or down depending on the intensity of the emotion it is experiencing.

Suggestions and strategies

When you are trying to help your child learn to express its emotions, you should avoid using expressions such as these: "What you are really feeling is that . . ."; "I think your expectations are too high in this situation . . ."; or "I guess you can see now that it was your own fault. . . ." Such expressions do not encourage the child to learn to register, categorize, and verbalize its sea of emotions.

Example

Six-year-old Rose is very good at registering, categorizing, and verbalizing her emotions. When her father falls ill and does not have the energy to interact with Rose anymore, she becomes angry and sad because she is used to her father being attentive and affectionate towards her. Fortunately, her father recovers, and she says to him: "I've been so angry with you because I was sad and I missed you. But it helped to be angry, it made it easier to bear."

MODEL **THE EMOTIONAL COMPASS**

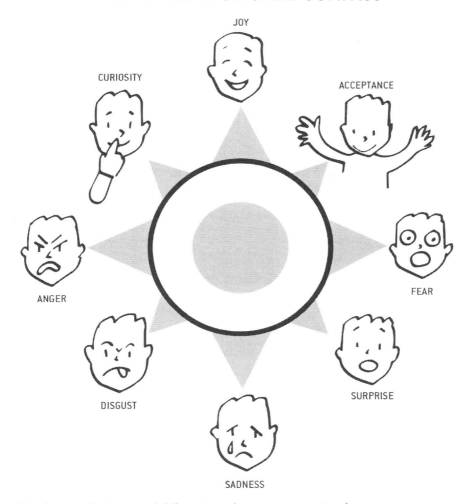

You have to help your child's notions become categorized emotions

Figure 4.9

How do you do it?

- Look at the compass with your child and talk about the different emotions.
- When you have a quiet moment, take a look at the compass and reflect – are there any of these emotions that it is hard for you to deal with when you see them in your child?
- Pay attention to the small child's emotions. You can say things like: "Did that make you sad?" When the child is older, you can include more context and say things such as: "If it was me in that situation, it would have made me sad."
- Notice when your child expresses its emotions in words and encourage it: "It was really good that you told me how you feel."

Regulating emotions – the volume button

In addition to verbalizing and categorizing emotions, children also have to learn how to regulate their emotions. Emotions can be viewed as a volume button – you experience an emotion with an intensity between 1 and 10. Sometimes you need to dial the emotion down a bit and other times you need to turn it up a notch. The most important thing is to learn to control your volume button. Emotion regulation develops from being externally regulated by the grown-up to being increasingly internally regulated by the child as it grows older and practices turning the volume up and down.

It is important that the child is allowed to practice regulating its emotions. It is like learning to drive a car – you need to go on the skidpan to practice the tumultuous and difficult situations. At the beginning, it seems hopeless, but if you are allowed to practice and to make mistakes you will eventually get really good at it – and even master the small, fine details.

Suggestions and strategies

It can be a good idea to introduce the emotional volume button to your child. Explain to the child that sometimes you need to be able to turn the volume up or down. Even grown-ups sometimes need someone to help them turn it up or down. It is great to be able to do it on your own and to know who to go to for help when it becomes too difficult. Show the compass to the child and tell it about situations featuring different levels of emotions, preferably from your own life.

Example

Nine-year-old Mike has been eating homemade cookies at his aunt's house. Unfortunately, he has eaten so many that he feels nauseous. In the bathroom, he sticks a finger down his throat and vomits, but at the same time he loses one of his remaining baby teeth. Blood and tooth come out along with the vomit. This made Mike so scared that later, just thinking about the situation makes him lose his appetite. In the following weeks he loses a lot of weight. Mike's parents notice it and nervously keep an eye on him during dinner time. They both repeat to him: "You have to eat!" Things continue to get out of hand.

The parents sit down to talk to Mike about it. They explain to him that if you have experienced something scary, it can easily make you dial your emotions all the way up when something reminds you of it, and that is what has happened to Mike when it comes to eating. But there was nothing dangerous about the experience he had, so he needs to turn down the volume. His mother has learned to do the same when she sees a spider.

MODEL VOLUME BUTTON

Figure 4.10

How do you do it?

- Every emotion has a volume button. Figure 4.9 illustrates the one for anger.
- Remember that you are your child's role model when it comes to learning to regulate emotions by turning the volume button up or down.
- In order to be able to regulate your child, you need to regulate yourself first – be in control of your own volume button.
- Regulate yourself through physical exercise or relaxing.
- Sometimes, emotions need to be regulated to a higher intensity – turn it up a notch.
- Sometimes, emotions need to be regulated to a lower intensity – dial it down.
- When helping your child regulate its emotions, it is a good idea to use non-verbal signals such as touch, empathic facial expressions, a soothing tone of voice, small sounds such as "mhm," "hmm," and "shhh," and to listen without judging.
- During times of peace, talk to the child about what it should do when it feels that its emotions are becoming too intense, such as asking a grown-up for help, thinking about its cat, or counting to 10.

Complex emotions

Emotions often have a complex structure (Allen et al. 2010). Part of learning to understand your emotions is to realize that emotions can be both interwoven and at odds with each other. It is possible to feel angry at your friends for not wanting to play with you and upset that you were left out at the same time. Perhaps you also feel jealous, which is a complex emotion. A way to deal with this is to be able to put complex emotions into words. Having a rich vocabulary for emotional states allows you to nuance as well as forming a comprehensive view of the confusing situation that arises when several conflicting emotions are at work at the same time. In addition, a rich vocabulary for complex emotions can make it easier for you to explain to others what you are feeling.

Figure 4.10 suggests how you can talk about the various emotions that pull you in different directions. The illustration is only meant as an inspiration for talking about emotions and does not contain all emotions. When interacting with your child, it is a good idea to use different terms for different emotions, as it encourages the child to also different emotional states as well.

Suggestions and strategies

When the child experiences very intense emotions, it can be hard for it to explain what it is feeling. The more painful and intense the emotional state, the less the child usually wants to talk about emotions.

Example

Eleven-year-old Ben is spending the night at his school as part of a social event. He is very nervous about it, and the week leading up to the event, he is unable to sleep. He needs his parents to talk to him about feeling scared, nervous, and unsure; having expectations; being irritated with yourself; and feeling ashamed of your own insecurity.

MODEL **COMPLEX EMOTIONS**

Figure 4.11

How do you do it?

- Look at the illustrations together and talk about situations when the child has experienced the different emotions. Begin by giving an example about yourself.
- You can encourage the child to draw a picture, and together you can come up with stories about the different emotions.

- Read aloud to the child from books that fit with the child's interests. The best children's literature emphasizes emotions.
- When you watch movies and TV series together, focus on the emotions expressed by the characters.
- Encourage the child to write a diary – and keep your hands off it!
- Use monologues – by telling short stories about the child or about other children, you let them know which emotions you imagine that the child is experiencing (see p. 204).
- Let the child browse for music that represents its various emotions.
- Look through magazines for different emotions.

Chapter 5

Your own childhood's influence on your parenting style and the mentalizing family

Our own childhood can be re-enacted in our relations to our children, and it is important to be able to change certain patterns of behaviour but also to be able to forgive yourself when you fall back into such patterns. This is the focus of Chapter 5. In order to create a mentalizing family, you must know what you are shaped by. That is, you need to be aware of your own background and your own baggage as a parent. Mentalizing parenting is characterized by the understanding that behaviour has underlying causes.

This chapter focuses on the mentalizing family viewed in the light of parents' own experiences with being part of a family, and what this means for the new family they are co-creating. We have decided to use research on the mentalizing relationship and the mentalizing family as our starting point. One way to talk about families is to focus one's attention on what makes a good family. In one way or another, everyone has been a part of a family, observed our own parents, and, as children, been unable to question whether this was the best way to parent. We easily come to recreate what we were used to at home, or else do everything we can to avoid recreating it.

Families develop structures to handle challenges and conflicts automatically, as a way to ensure predictability and security. However, these structures can also be harmful, because they can shut down opportunities for flexibility and development. Keeping experiences from our own family close in mind makes us blind to ourselves and our own children. Therefore, it can be a good idea to examine your own family with the use of some analytical models. The family structures that are represented in this chapter are suggestions as to the ways in which you can look at and structure a family. The models allow you to take an observer's view at yourself and your family, which can serve as a starting point for a conversation about hierarchies and boundaries between the members of the family.

Caring adults in one's childhood – angels in the nursery

"Angels in the nursery" refers to the positive stories/people that you remember from your childhood as an adult. Our angels in the nursery are mental images of people who were good to us when we were growing up. These memories can help us feel safe, just by remembering them. It can be people who were kind and caring towards you or who helped you through a difficult time in your childhood – people you could rely on when everything seemed hopeless or people who were able to identify the underlying reasons for bad behaviour and who always loved you unconditionally.

Suggestions and strategies

Angels also come in the form of religious figures or animals. When we look for angels, we do it to form mental images that can help us find the people who have made us feel valuable and have instilled in us the motivation to continue developing ourselves.

Example

When Mary was a child, she had a close relationship with her grandmother. Her grandmother was the one who understood her, and she always had time and energy for Mary. She believed in her and listened to her. Mary's own mother worked a lot, and Mary often felt that she let her down. Fortunately, she had her grandmother. When Mary became a mother herself to twin girls, she expected her mother to be like her grandmother. However, her mother, who is now retired, is full of energy and busy with a lot of activities. Mary feels very disappointed, but she understands that her grandmother was the angel in her nursery who helped her understand what it means to be a good, dependable attachment figure. She also understands that you cannot pass on role expectations between generations. Rather than sitting back and passively waiting for someone else to take on the role as her children's angel, she needs to actively take it upon herself.

MODEL **ANGELS IN THE NURSERY**

Figure 5.1

How do you do it?

Think back on your own childhood and fill the angel with drawings or words about the people who were most significant to you.

Mother

> Do you remember the adults who were particularly supportive to you during your childhood?

_____

> Do you have any memories that are particularly good, where you felt that you were met with an open mind?

_____

> Who was it easiest for you to talk to when you were a teenager?

_____

Father

Do you remember the adults who were particularly supportive to you during your childhood?

_____

Do you have any memories that are particularly good, where you felt that you were met with an open mind?

_____

Who was it easiest for you to talk to when you were a teenager?

_____

Negative experiences in one's childhood – ghosts in the nursery

Ghosts symbolize negative events in one's childhood. When it comes to traumatic events, humans have a memory like an elephant – and an elephant remembers extremely well. In evolutionary terms, this makes sense, because remembering something dangerous enables you to avoid it in the future, which ensures one's survival. Like ghosts, such experiences can haunt us and affect the way we interact with our children. If the ghosts are set free and laid to rest, they will not come back to haunt us as parents and cast their shadow upon us. Instead, mentalizing conversations can transform them into safely buried ancestors. You might say that "what can be share, we can bear"

Suggestions and strategies

People protect themselves and do not revisit their ghosts if they are not ready. Do not put pressure on your partner, but by being gentle and interested, you can encourage them to want to look at their ghosts.

Example

A mother and a father are sitting with their newborn child, who is screaming. The father grew up with his own father's fits of rage and a mother who was controlling and fault finding. During his childhood, his father often became too angry, after which his mother would lecture him on his failings as a father.

Back in the present, the parents are able to comfort their little boy. They talk about the ghosts in the nursery, what their own childhood was like, and what sort of parents they would like to be. They find that it helps to express it into words. However, when their son tests their limit later that night and they are unable to comfort him, the ghosts still turn up.

The father yells: "Don't you see that he's hungry – start feeding him!" and the mother answers: "You are ruining our son, just as your father did." Time and time again they must sit down together in peacetime to talk about the ghosts and lay them to rest, and to forgive themselves and each other for their reappearance.

MODEL **GHOSTS IN THE NURSERY**

What can be shared can be cured

Figure 5.2

How do you do it?

Think back on your own childhood and fill the ghost with drawings or words about events that scared you or left you feeling intensely abandoned.

Mother

Do you remember feeling scared when you were growing up?

_____

What is the worst, most humiliating, or most lonely experience you remember from your childhood?

_____

Who made you feel most insecure when you were a child, and why?

_____

Father

Do you remember feeling scared when you were growing up?

What is the worst, most humiliating, or most lonely experience you remember from your childhood?

Who made you feel most insecure and anxious when you were a child, and why?

Repetition compulsion

Repetition compulsion occurs when parents are stressed and act without thinking, and almost compulsively repeat negative behaviour that originates in their own childhood (Freud 1917). Today, we understand repetition compulsion as a range of dynamics that, when combined, can explain the process (Thimmer & Hagelquist 2017).

The first dynamic is the repetition compulsion itself, which is simply the way people learn. As small children, we repeatedly drop our pacifier over the edge of the baby carriage to understand how gravity works. So, when parents repeat what they saw their own parent do, they do it in order to understand what happened when they were children themselves. The second dynamic is the wish for control. Nothing can make us feel as powerless as our children. For instance, if you saw that your parents used violence to gain control, you will be more likely to use the same technique yourself. The third dynamic consists of the fact that the purpose of the repetition compulsion is to regulate emotions. When your child makes you feel angry, sad, or scared, you want to regulate those intense emotions. When you repeat a behaviour, then, it is part of an effort to gain control, but it also indicates that one's ability to regulate emotions is not fully developed. The final dynamic of repetition compulsion has to do with habits. People love habits because it is easier to do what we always do. When we feel stressed there is an even greater risk that we will resort to habits.

Together, these dynamics create vicious spirals that repeat themselves, resulting in a rankling sense of insecurity and lack of control rather than learning. They are easily started when our children make us feel insecure or powerless. Basically, repetition compulsion has to do with the fact that we tend to act in the same way that our own caregivers did, but unconsciously we hope to meet someone who will act differently and from them learn that things can work out differently. That experience will help you heal.

Suggestions and strategies

Be curious and investigative when you notice that you repeat your parents' adverse behaviour. Talk to your partner about the origins of your repetitive patterns. This will make it easier for your partner to understand you. Understanding leads to learning, which enables you to develop new strategies.

Example

When Ryan was a child and his father was angry with him, he would punish him by giving him the silent treatment. The silence could last for days. Ryan hated it and did everything he could to avoid making his father angry or disappointed. He wants to be a good father to his two sons, but when he gets angry, he instinctively tries to control the emotion by falling silent and pulling away like his own father did. One day, Ryan's eldest son, who is 5 years old, says to him: "I'm sorry I was bad. Please talk to me again?" Ryan recognizes the pattern from his own upbringing and resolves to work on avoiding this type of repetition compulsion.

MODEL **REPETITION COMPULSION**

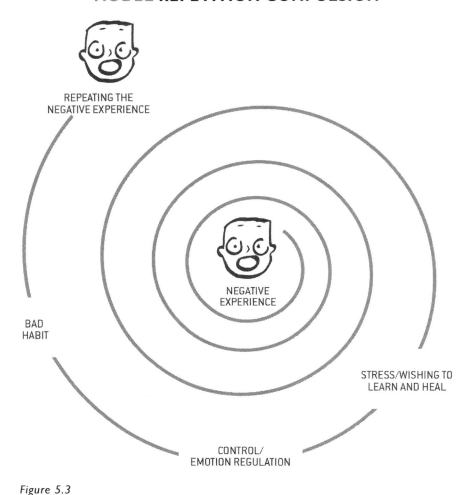

Figure 5.3

How do you do it?

Which patterns of behaviour do you tend to repeat in relation to your child that you saw your mother do, which you did not think were supportive or encouraging for your development at that time?

Which patterns of behaviour do you tend to repeat in relation to your child that you saw your father do, which you did not think were supportive or encouraging for your development at that time?

Are there any situations in which you are especially likely to experience repetition compulsion?

_____

How do you react in these situations?

_____

How do you feel afterwards?

_____

Overcoming trauma and negative experiences

There is only one way to overcome trauma or negative experiences/ghosts from one's childhood – to learn to recognize and understand from them. You can do this by talking about it with your partner, your friends, or a psychologist. Mentalizing conversations enables you to capture the ghosts and transform them into safely buried ancestors.

Suggestions and strategies

Complete the exercises on repetition compulsion, angels, and ghosts. Return to look at them when you notice earlier patterns of behaviour repeating themselves in your present interaction with your child.

Example

Alice's sister drowned when they were children. Now, she is constantly afraid that something will happen to her little daughter. In particular, she is terrified of anything involving water. Her daughter has picked up on her mother's signals, and as a consequence she is afraid to go to swimming pools and to the beach. However, she has also developed a general fear of being away from her mother, which has developed into school phobia because she is afraid to leave her mother.

MODEL OVERCOMING TRAUMA AND NEGATIVE EXPERIENCES

Figure 5.4

How do you do it?

Visualize the ghosts being laid to rest. An example could be to go to your childhood home to say goodbye to the ghosts. You can also keep this page with your notes and let it be a part of your personal history.

Have there been any traumatic or negative experiences in your life?

_____

_____

Do you have any examples of how they affect you today?

_____

_____

Have there been situations where you notice that you repeat patterns of behaviour that would have been useful during the traumatic event but are disadvantageous today?

_____

_____

Is there a way to symbolically bury these ghosts?

_____

_____

Are there any difficult experiences or relationships from your childhood that you worry will affect your role as a parent?

_____

_____

Creating a learning environment when interaction is difficult

In this section, we examine the best way to create an environment of calm and reflection that allows you to set boundaries in a way that encourages learning and the child's ability to mentalize (Siegel & Bryson 2014). Originally, discipline meant to learn or to give instruction. When you are raising a child, the most important thing is to teach the child the things it is not yet able to do – not to punish it.

Suggestions and strategies

Thinking about learning and using a structure such as "why? – what? – how?" can help you focus and thereby avoid falling into the trap of "mentalization failure."

Example

It is Friday night, and a tired mother is watching her child, who is lying on the floor of the supermarket, screaming. They are having a conflict about how much money her daughter should have for candy. At first, the mother instinctively thinks: "My daughter needs discipline." But then she remembers to use "why? – what? – how?" to regulate intense emotions and to "discipline."

Why is my daughter acting this way? Is it because she has been looking forward to Friday all week because she is allowed to have candy? What does she need me to teach her? That it is nice to look forward to something and that sometimes you can have too much of a good thing. How do I teach her that? The mother kneels next to her daughter and tells her that candy is great in moderation, but unhealthy if you eat too much. They talk about delayed gratification and that sometimes in life you can't always get what you want. And that sometimes it is a great feeling to look forward to something – such as Christmas.

MODEL CREATING A LEARNING ENVIRONMENT WHEN INTERACTION IS DIFFICULT

Figure 5.5

Source: Authors' adaptation (Siegel & Bryson 2014)

How do you do it?

When you find yourself in a situation where you child is testing boundaries or is experiencing mentalization failure, try to raise yourself above the situation and think "why? – what? – how?"

* Why is he acting this way right now?
* What does he need me to teach him?
* How do I teach him that?

Then it is a question of will or won't. Does he want to learn, or is he unable to learn at the moment?

What kind of parent do you want to be when interaction is difficult?

* Which values are important for you to pass on to your child?
* What kind of role model do you want to be to your child?
* What is it important that your child learns?

Reflections for difficult situations

- Why do you think the situation progressed the way it did?
- How did you feel/what were you thinking when it was most difficult?
- What was going on in your child's mind?
- Think about the last time you lost the ability to mentalize with your child — was there anything in particular that triggered you? How did you feel? What were you thinking?
- Do you recognize this pattern from other situations?

Triggers in parent–child interaction

A trigger is an event/situation/emotion that reminds you of previous negative experiences and activates intense emotions such as anxiety, anger, or stress. Humans have an alarm system that triggers us when we are in danger. This alarm system is useful, and it has helped us survive through the ages. When the alarm goes off, your body prepares to react. It gives us energy to fight, flee, or freeze. Once we have experienced a danger, we will be on guard if we meet with the same triggers again.

As parents, you bring your own baggage into your interaction with your children. In some situations, you might be triggered by something that has nothing to do with the child. When your child refuses to do as they are told, it can activate feelings of powerlessness that you used to feel as a child when your parents used force. Often, the triggers we experience when interacting with our children is false alarm. For example when we hear, see, or feel something that reminds us of something that once happened (Blaustein & Kinniburgh 2010).

Trigger-analysis is used to analyze a specific situation and can be used both in relation to yourself and your child. What was the actual behaviour? Which internal triggers (emotions, thoughts, etc.) and external (other people's behaviour etc.) preceded the behaviour? Which emotions did you or your child experience in the situation, and what were the underlying reasons for the behaviour?

Suggestions and strategies

It is a good idea to familiarize yourself with the things that trigger you in relation to your child. Usually, your child has unconsciously noticed it. Make sure to carefully consider which strategies you want to use when you are triggered.

Example

A father who was bullied as a child recalls his childhood. He remembers feeling helpless and especially the way it felt when the others laughed at him and he did not understand why. One night, he is driving his teenage daughter and her friends, whom he has always been on good terms with, to a party. The girls are singing along to music with the volume turned all the way up. One of the girls suggests that they find a song the father can sing along to. They pick out a very old song that starts to play in the car, and all the girls laugh loudly. The father stiffens instinctively and turns off the music system with an angry remark.

Immediately after, he senses the feelings of helplessness and of not fitting in that he felt as a child. The following day, the father still wants to understand what happened and finds the following trigger analysis. By going through the analysis, he traces the causal relations behind the emotions he felt as a child. The next time he drives the girls to a party, he will pay more attention and be more reflective about his own reactions.

MODEL TRIGGERS IN PARENT–CHILD INTERACTION

Trigger inner/ outer (internal/ external) (What triggered the beha-viour, what happened?)	Behavior (Describe the behavior, what did you do?)	Emotions (Which emotions were you experiencing?)	Reasons What were the reasons for reacting the way you did?

Figure 5.6

How do you do it?

Use the table "Triggers in parent–child interaction" to analyze what triggers you or your child in specific situations.

Crisis plan

In order to be proactive when it comes to handling difficult situations, it can be a good idea to analyze them in peacetime. You can do it alone or together as parents. The point is that in peacetime, you are able to see how you can regulate yourself and notice other possible lines of action that you are blind to at times when emotions are intense and difficult to regulate.

Developing a crisis management plan is a mentalizing task in itself. Think about a particularly difficult situation involving your child. Remember to be as specific as possible. What exactly happened? Where were you? What was going on inside you? You must continuously evaluate and adjust the crisis management plan to your experiences. A difficult situation can serve as the basis for development. When developing a crisis management plan, you talk about emotions as the reason for behaviour, and it will show you that certain emotions do not automatically lead to certain behaviours. Working with a crisis management plan will give you and your child new experiences.

Suggestions and strategies

The plan for crisis management can take the form of a card that can be tucked into your pocket or as notes on your phone. It must contain concrete directions for how you should behave when emotions run high.

Example

A father has a hard time handling it when his teenage daughter talks down to him. She might say things like: "Why should I clean up when you're always acting as a maid around here anyway?" He becomes so angry that he yells things at her that he regrets immediately afterwards. He is especially sorry when he reacts by yelling that he really wishes that she would move out soon so he wouldn't have to look at her anymore. He makes a crisis management plan which makes him realize that he is triggered because he feels humiliated.

He wonders whether it is possible to choose another line of action rather than shouting. He recalls that when he becomes irritated with a colleague at work, he focuses his attention on his phone until he has regulated himself. Afterwards, he is able to calmly talk to his colleague about his feelings. He applies this strategy to the difficult situations with his daughter, and it helps him regulate himself and talk to her about better ways to communicate. After all, it is a bad habit to talk that way to the people you live with and care about.

MODEL **CRISIS PLAN**

In which situations is there a special risk of things going wrong?

_____

_____

Which emotions do you find it especially difficult to handle (anger, sadness, anxiety, feeling abandoned)?

_____

_____

Do you have any previous experience with reacting differently in the situation, avoiding the behaviour at the root of the crisis management plan?

_____

_____

What can you do in similar situations in the future instead of behaving in the way that led you to form a crisis management plan?

_____

_____

What do you think might help you when you are about to behave the way that led you to form a crisis management plan?

_____

_____

How do you regulate emotions in other situations? What do you normally do when you feel angry or sad?

_____

_____

Who can you contact or ask for help when you are about to behave the way that led you to form a crisis management plan?

_____

_____

Figure 5.7

An open mind – the thermometer

When interacting with children who are experiencing intense emotions, your job as a parent is to act as a kind of thermostat that sets the desired emotional temperature. This way, parents become role models who show the child that emotional states can be regulated through reflection. It is important to have the self-awareness to see when you are unable to interact with your child in a way that supports development. If possible, you may ask the other parent – who is not experiencing the same degree of emotional intensity and who is therefore able to mentalize – to deal with the situation.

Suggestions and strategies

If you use the thermometer shortly after a difficult situation in which you have experienced mentalization failure, it can help you become aware of how it works – to see when you are able to reflect and when you are not. Begin by asking yourself the questions in the thermometer consistently, but in time, you should let it become an automatic process when you are experiencing intense emotions.

Example

A mother is heading to her teenager's room to tell her how frustrated she is that, once again, she has had to clean up in the kitchen after her daughter has cooked a meal for herself. Right before she enters her daughter's room, she takes her own temperature to make sure she has an open mind for the conversation. She notices that she is too full of her own emotions, so she asks the father to take over. He finds a quiet moment to go to his daughter's room and sits down on her bed. They have a good talk about what it means to be a part of a family and that they have to be "on the same side" in order for things to work. He tells her why it is so important that everyone contributes to making the household work and that loading the dishes is just one of many things that the adults are taking care of to make things run smoothly. His teenage daughter understands, she just hasn't realized it before. Usually, the dishes seem to just "disappear of their own accord."

MODEL **AN OPEN MIND – THE THERMOMETER**

On a scale from 1–10, how intense are my emotions? _____

Am I open to seeing things from other perspectives?

_____

_____

Have I found a balance between the pressure to act and being reflective?

_____

_____

Am I able to feel empathy towards myself and the other person?

_____

_____

Am I genuinely curious about the mental states that lie behind the behaviour?

_____

_____

Do I have the time and patience to handle the situation properly?

_____

_____

Figure 5.8

How do you do it?

Think about the thermometer as a tool for determining whether you are able to enter into a mentalization interaction here and now.

The family community

When a child is born, it takes many helpers to support and encourage the child's development. The greater the number of people involved in raising a child, the more resources are available to the child. The expression: "It takes a village to raise a child" means that a child needs many adults in its life to survive, understand the surrounding culture, and develop its potentials: family members, teachers, neighbours, and friends who ensure that the child develops and thrives.

Psychologists used to place the greatest emphasis on the relationship between mother and child. Today, many studies on the relationship between father and child have concluded that from the beginning, the father's relation to the child is essential – not just for the child but for the new family as a whole (Feldman 2007). When the father partakes in changing diapers, comforting, and tucking the child in, he experiences an increase in the parenting hormone (oxytocin), while there is a decrease in hormones associated with dominance and aggression (Cabrera et al. 2014). Research has also demonstrated the importance of the father taking an active role in relation to his child, as it has a positive effect on the mother's stress level as well as the new family's sense of cohesion and belonging. A family is established quickly, and it can be hard to change these early patterns at a later time.

By looking at the family's social relations and resources, it is possible to recognize all the resources that are available not only in one's partner but in other family members, as well as more distant relations. Look to your close relations, grandparents, teachers, neighbours, and friends.

Suggestions and strategies

Things do not always turn out the way you might have wanted. However, that does not mean that everything is lost if your child does not have a father or there are not as many relations and family members around the child as you would like. Remember that you have a long life ahead of you and that things are seldom as perfect as you might wish for.

Example

A family has just arrived home from the hospital with their newborn son. It was a difficult birth, and they had trouble getting the breastfeeding on track. It is hard for the mother to let go of her new son, and she thinks her partner is too clumsy in the way he is handling the child. She does not like her mother-in-law to hold the boy because she is a smoker, and the mother hates it when her son smells of tobacco when she gets him back. She is also irritated with her own mother because she can see that she doesn't like the boy's name.

It is a great help for her when she is finally able to put all of her emotions into words while she also attempts to let go a little bit and let others take care of her son. When she talks to her partner about how afraid she is of letting go of her responsibility, it makes them understand each other better. They agree that they should both work on helping her let go of control a little bit, while he should also learn to listen to her advice.

MODEL THE FAMILY COMMUNITY

Figure 5.9

How do you do it?

When you let your partner participate, you give your child a great gift:

- You let your partner's brain develop to become more caring.
- You reduce your own risk of stress.
- What you are doing now affects the patterns you establish for the future.
- As a partner to someone who has a hard time letting go, remember that they do not act from ill will. Usually, it is a matter of anxiety and inse-curity, so listen, be respectful, and show your partner that you are able to help her.
- If you are a single parent, try to include others as carers for your child.

When you allow your family and other people who are close to you to form a relation to your child, you give your child a great gift:

- You give your child the chance to be surrounded by many people who can help it develop and thrive.
- Your child has more caregivers who can make it feel safe and secure.
- You make your closest relations feel involved and committed to help you and your child in the future.

The relationship – the space between the couple

The relationship is the space in which the family lives and develops when two become three. Having a baby greatly changes your life, and it is easy to forget to devote attention to the relationship. Research (Gottman 1999) has shown that couples who do well are good at solving conflicts, and they are good at adding vitamins to their relationship in between conflicts.

The space between the couple is the playground for the relationship as well as for the child. If the couple do not devote enough attention to their relationship, they will gradually start to pollute the space between them. A polluted space creates anxiety in the couple – and the child who breathes in it. When space and attention is devoted to the relationship, the space is fertilized. It becomes a safe and good place to be, and the safer the space between the couple is, the easier it is to be mentalizing and resolve conflicts by crossing the gangway to each other – that is, to sincerely try to understand what is going on in the other person's mind.

We know that many marital conflicts cannot be solved, but those couples who do best are able to live with their differences and acknowledge their partner's perspective. Couples who turn towards each other instead of away from each other when things are difficult have a better chance of working through the problem. These couples know that in order to solve the conflict they must talk about their disagreements in a calm, respectful way – that is, to fertilize the space between them. They also know that criticism and reproaches contaminate the space, quickly neutralizing appreciation.

Suggestions and strategies

A successful relationship is not the one in which the partners agree on everything – rather, it is the one where the partners are able to understand the rationale and the intention behind the other person's behaviour and create a shared world in which both parties are aware that many conflicts must be accepted rather than solved.

Example

Since becoming a mother, Grace has felt extremely anxious, especially since her 6-month-old daughter has started to crawl in addition to not sleeping well. Grace reacts by taking it out on her husband, saying: "You can't help me anyway. I have to take care of everything." This provokes the husband, who wants to do everything he can to support his wife and be a good father. His immediate reaction is to turn away from her, and he automatically thinks: "Whatever, she can suit herself." Instead, however, he turns to her and suggests that they sit down to talk about what he can do to help her.

When their daughter is finally asleep, he listens to his wife telling him about the huge pressure she is under. She also tells him that the reason why she snapped at him was that she actually needed his help and support because she has been feeling so overwhelmed. The husband wonders why she does not simply tell him what she needs. However, he is glad because he wants to help her. He also explains to her that when he sometimes tends to step aside, it is only because he thinks Grace is a brilliant mother and he is afraid that he will not be able to do it as well as her.

MODEL THE RELATIONSHIP

Figure 5.10

How do you do it?

Fertilizing the space

Make it a priority to sit down together once a week after the children are asleep. One of you crosses the gangway to the other person's mind as they tell about something they have appreciated in the other and what it means. The first person's job is simply to listen and repeat what has been said using the same words. Then you switch.

The four encounters

Over the course of a day, there are at least four stages of transition for a couple: when we look at each other after we wake up, when we leave for work, when we meet later in the day, and when we go to bed.

Do you take the time to properly greet and say goodbye to each other? If these moments are characterized by too much haste and a lack of attention, it can contaminate the space. By focusing on these four encounters during the day, you make it safer and easier to establish a good contact. You do this by keeping the mind in mind and maintaining an open mind.

Crossing the gangway can sometimes feel like having a steel cable or a thick elastic band attached to your back that keeps trying to pull you back — it is a difficult but important exercise to be able to cross the gangway to the other person. Furthermore, in doing so, we exercise our mentalizing muscle.

Created in collaboration with Lone Algot Jeppesen, psychologist and specialist in psychotherapy.

The mentalizing family

The family is a very special social group. It has structures and rules, and during its lifetime, it faces a range of developmental tasks (Minuchin 1978) such as securing its own survival and supporting each other. In the family, there must be room for development and learning for adults as well as children, and it must be able to adapt to changes in the family members and the surrounding environment. It is also in the family that we must learn to manage intense emotions and run the risk of experiencing mentalization failure.

No one can do everything perfectly on the first try – and being part of a mentalizing family is first and foremost about trusting in your own, your partner's, and your children's ability to grow and develop. The purpose of a mentalizing family – aside from ensuring survival and development – is to provide clearly defined limits and boundaries, but also to create flexibility.

When you are not hung up on a single perspective, it is possible to take a playful approach characterized by warmth, kindness, and humour. The ambition of the mentalizing family is that problem solving and conflict resolution take place in a process characterized by mutual respect for each other's viewpoint. Trust and humility are also essential. Mentalizing parents are preoccupied with registering and discovering good mentalization and praising it when they encounter it (Asen & Fonagy 2011).

Suggestions and strategies

In all families, there are times when the members are not as mentalizing and well-adapted to the challenges that arise as they would wish. In fact, it is a sign of health that things do not always follow a straight line, but we encourage you to use the following examples as inspiration for ways to moderate the environment and structures of the family. Using terminology from the nautical universe, you might say that you need to have a healthy marine environment that is inviting and encourages development and in which you know the rules and know who you should apply to for help.

Example

A divorced mother of two teenage daughters has met a new man, and it is increasingly difficult for them to find a way to create a family together. The new man has a son who is nearly grown, calm, and well-adjusted, while the woman has two wild teenage daughters. The man has a very specific idea about what it means to be a family, and he feels that his son is proof that his way is the right way. The woman's concept of family is very different from the family he created with his ex-wife. The following models helped them reflect on what kind of family they wanted to be. In particular, it became clear that families are different because they are made up of different people, and it is important to adapt the family to the individual members of the group.

MODEL **THE MENTALIZING FAMILY**

Figure 5.11

How do you do it?

A mentalizing family:

- Has room for learning and development.
- Is able to adapt to outside circumstances.
- Is able to adapt as the family members grow and evolve.
- Has members that are attached to each other.
- Is conscious that attachment leads to intense emotions and a risk of mentalization failure.
- Places hope and trust in the other members' abilities to develop and change.
- Sets clearly defined limits and boundaries but is also flexible.
- Is not set in a certain way of thinking.
- Sees problem solving and conflicts as elements of a process in which there is mutual respect for each other's viewpoints.
- Is interested in mental states.
- Has parents that register and notice good mentalization and praises its presence.
- Continually works on trusting each other.

The family hierarchy

All groups have a hierarchy, and in the family group it is absolutely necessary. Ideally, parents are at the top of the hierarchy and possess decision-making competencies when it comes to assigning roles and providing clearly defined limits for the family. This makes sense in terms of the mindset that parenthood is all about learning, as this position allows parents to take care of their child, pass on knowledge, and encourage the child to realize its full mental potential.

Preferably, at the top of the hierarchy, parents rank alongside each other and support each other: They try to understand each other's perspectives so they are aligned in terms of values and rules. Parents have integrity and boundaries without being too rigid and detached. They are able to provide a framework that allows for the family to solve any problems or conflicts that may arise in a mentalizing way.

Even for an ideal family, the teenage years are going to be particularly difficult when it comes to the parents staying on top of the hierarchy, but that is completely normal. Teenagers experiment with being adults and eventually being in charge of their own family. If you ask teenagers where they rank in the family hierarchy, they will typically say that they are at the top (Björnör 2016).

It is inadvisable to turn the hierarchy upside down, putting the parents' needs in front of the children's. At worst, children will feel that it is their responsibility to take care of the physical and emotional needs of the adults. Preferably, the parents are at the top of the hierarchy, but they must also be flexible. When the 10-year-old is better at reading a map than his parents when the family is on a mountain hike, the 10-year-old decides which way to go. When the teenager grows older, it can sometimes be a good idea to let him or her take the same position in the hierarchy as the parents. At other times, parents must retain their elevated position.

Suggestions and strategies

Think about the hierarchy as a position to impart knowledge. If you do not have this position, we suggest that you return to Chapter 1, in which power and epistemic trust were described.

Example

A father grew up in a family with a strict family hierarchy. In his own role as a parent, he wants to find a softer version of the family structure from his childhood. He has succeeded in listening to and embracing his children and their development. However, he is challenged by his teenage daughter. When planning a family vacation, all his suggestions are rejected, and his daughter keeps changing her attitude from not wanting to go to suggesting new destinations.

After having discussed the issue for a long time, in which the father has attempted to accommodate his daughter in the process, he feels that his boundaries have been overstepped in terms of the roles of adult and children. He and his wife decide that the family will take a trip to the coast during the holiday. To everyone's surprise, the daughter conforms to the family hierarchy.

MODEL THE FAMILY HIERARCHY

Parents at the top of the hierarchy   Children at the top of the hierarchy

Figure 5.12

How do you do it?

*   In general, parents should be at the top of the hierarchy.
*   The hierarchy might look different for individual reasons: the child's age, competencies, or special situations.

The following questions can be used to encourage reflection on the family hierarchy:

*   What does your family hierarchy look like – who is at the top?
*   Are there any alliances between the mother or the father and the children that influence the hierarchy, and is this a good idea?
*   Do the parents use their position in the hierarchy to create a mentalizing family environment?
*   Do the parents have the necessary authority? Do the children need limits and guidance? Are the children asked to make decisions that make them feel insecure, helpless, or incompetent?
*   Do the parents use their children as pawns in their discussions (triangulation) and put them in a no-win situation in which they have to choose between their parents?

The family – external boundaries

The family is the first group that the child becomes a part of, and it is the first place for the child to learn how a group works. The family group constitutes a group because it has boundaries that set the family apart as a unit and define who is a part of the group, and how. Families vary in terms of the flexibility of these boundaries, and therefore also in their degree of cohesion and openness towards their surroundings.

According to Minuchin (1978), the ideal family has transparent boundaries (cf. the illustration in Figure 5.13 drawn with a dotted line). It is character-ized by a sense of belonging and a sense that external boundaries exist, but the family is also open to its surroundings. Each family member feels that they are part of a group. There might be a certain structure, but there is also openness. Others are welcome, but there is a distinct feeling that "we" belong together.

A family whose external boundaries are closed tend to direct their focus inwards. Curiosity towards the surrounding world might be replaced with reserve and perhaps even animosity towards intruders. Family members who experiment with forming relations outside the family or who develop interest and enthusiasm about other family structures are met with coldness and anger.

A family whose external boundaries are wide open might feel a sense of detachment from one another. The family does not really have any bounda-ries – the family members are free as air; the parents are disengaged from their role and allow the children to do as they please. Perhaps there are no fixed mealtimes, and the older children can stay with another family for days without anyone taking notice.

External boundaries can be drawn when a family experiences that others have spoken ill of them. On the other hand, negative experiences such as ill-ness, stress, or a lack of energy to unite the family can blur the family's external boundaries.

Suggestions and strategies

Usually, you structure your own family based on your experiences in the first family group you were a part of. Sit down alone or as a couple to take a critical look at your family and explore how your individual experiences and personal histories influence the way in which you structure the new family you have created together.

Example

A family with closed external boundaries is living on a quiet residential street. In winter, the children are playing with other children from the street before heading back home at dinnertime. At the dinner table, their father talks about an argument he has had with their neighbour about snow removal. He is very upset and has told off the neighbour for not clearing away a pile of snow that blocks his driveway. He interrupts the children, who are excitedly relating their day of fun, playing in the snow with the other children, and exclaims: "They are all raving idiots next door who do just as they please with no concern for others, and so I've told them. I'll tell you kids; you better stay well clear of them!"

MODEL **EXTERNAL BOUNDARIES**

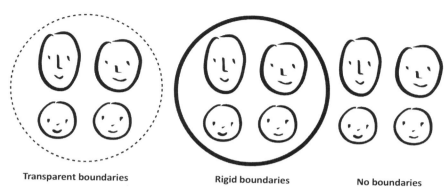

Transparent boundaries   Rigid boundaries   No boundaries

Figure 5.13

How do you do it?

- Look at your family as a unit, the status of your external boundaries, and your degree of external openness. Figure 5.11 distinguishes between transparent boundaries, boundaries that are hard and rigid, and no boundaries.
- In what ways do you see the family structure of your childhood influence the way you set boundaries for your own family today?
- What do other people say about your family and its external boundaries?
- How do you think your children would describe the way your family is today when they grow up?

The family – boundaries between family members

The way in which the family handles closeness and the right to autonomy and privacy is something that requires continual reflection. When it comes to boundaries between the individual members of a family, we distinguish between the things that are shared by the family and the things you do not share with your family because it is personal and private.

The ideal family is the balanced family who has flexible boundaries and a natural space between the family members (Figure 5.13 (dotted line)). Such a family has integrity and boundaries but is also open and generous. Its members have a right to personal boundaries – they are transparent about their mental states, but they also have a right to a private inner life.

In families where there are no boundaries between family members, you might experience mentalizing practices that cross individual boundaries (Figure 5.14). For instance, the mother might be certain that she knows exactly what her child is feeling and disapprove of secrets. Such a family might seem mentalizing, but more often than not, the absence of boundaries results in family members feeling lonely and misunderstood. You might be convinced that you know what is going on inside the other person's mind, but since you can never know for sure what the other person is experiencing, it may not be true.

In families with closed boundaries and great distance between the family members (Figure 5.13 (solid line)), the inner world of each individual member is entirely closed off from the others. You do not know what is going on with the others, and you do not talk about how they are feeling deep down. Parents and children keep to themselves, and there is a sense that what is going on inside my mind is none of your business.

Suggestions and strategies

As the child grows older, it will increasingly need its own private mental space. As a consequence, boundaries that used to be open will be closed. It is important that the family accommodates and respects the child during this process.

Example

In a family with children from different marriages, differences in terms of inner boundaries are clearly felt. The mother and her daughters are always in tune with each other, while the father and his sons maintain clear boundaries between each other when it comes to their emotions. The boys' mother has moved away and found a new boyfriend. The girls' mother is at a loss to understand why the boys' father does not ask them about how they are feeling about it. The father, however, insists that the boys have a right to their "space." In contrast, the mother talks to her children on the phone several times a day, and she always needs to know how they are feeling. She is convinced that they are sure to be upset and that they must need her – even when this is not the case. These differences in inner boundaries also manifest physically. When the laundry is done, the father carefully divides it into separate piles and places it neatly into his sons' individual wardrobes, which are clearly labelled. The mother and her daughters borrow each other's clothes and makeup and are far more boundary-free when it comes to sharing each other's thoughts and actions.

MODEL BOUNDARIES BETWEEN FAMILY MEMBERS

Natural boundaries – members are interested in each other's minds and respectful of each other's boundaries

No boundaries/symbiosis

Strong individual boundaries – no cohesion

Figure 5.14

How do you do it?

- As a rule, you should have the right to maintain individual boundaries, but you should not find yourselves so far apart that you are completely out of touch with each other.

- Consider how each individual member experiences the family boundaries.
- Make a drawing of the family to illustrate who are close to each other and who are far away from each other.
- Reflect on the boundaries together as parents and evaluate whether they are fine the way they are or if one of the family members is in need of more space and personal boundaries, or if they are too far away and that steps should be taken to bring them closer.

The family – internal boundaries

Internal boundaries refer to the mental boundaries and flexibility of each individual family member. When we experience intense emotions or feel that life is difficult, we have different ways of handling it. In this book, we use the language of mentalization to describe the way we react. In mentalization theory, our reaction to difficult circumstances is viewed as a boundary put up by the mind when it is too overwhelmed to mentalize. The terms used to describe these processes are far from simple, but the most important thing is not the terms themselves but to be able to understand and recognize it when you feel this way.

The term *teleological mode* refers to ways of thinking in which you resort to a very concrete understanding of things – in terms of parenting, you might think that when the child acts a certain way, it must learn from it through concrete and maybe even physical consequences.

The second way of reacting is called *psychic equivalence mode*. This refers to a way of thinking in which you assume that the way you perceive reality is automatically true. For example, if I think that the reason why my daughter does not want to do her homework, it is because she does not care about her life – and this is reality!

Lastly, *pretend mode* refers to a state of mind in which you are detached from reality. Your mental states do not correspond to reality in a flexible way. In this mode, the person might engage in "psychobabble": "I'll do anything for her, but because of her sensitive mind it is simply impossible for us to find our way to each other." When in pretend mode, people tend to intellectualize and not actually relate emotionally to the other person, and often express themselves in clichés.

Suggestions and strategies

Go over situations in your mind in which your internal boundaries were tested – what do you notice yourself experiencing? Do you see yourself fixing on a concrete, physical solution to the situation? Are you convinced that there is only one right way to perceive reality, namely yours? Or are you overwhelmed by theories and thoughts that prevent you from relating to what is going on in yourself and in your child?

Example

Amy and Brad's son Louis is born three months prematurely. He is very small and fragile, and vulnerable to infections. The new parents become overly focused on making sure that everything is properly washed and cleaned. They are hyperattentive to Louis' signals. He is doing fine, but when he starts to crawl, it is a huge challenge for both of his parents. Brad wants to babyproof everything, while Amy is frustrated and anxious. She convinces herself that Louis crawls away from her intentionally to vex her and is unable to see that it is a natural part of his development. Brad attempts to deal with the challenges teleologically, whilst Amy is fixed in psychic equivalence.

MODEL **INTERNAL BOUNDARIES**

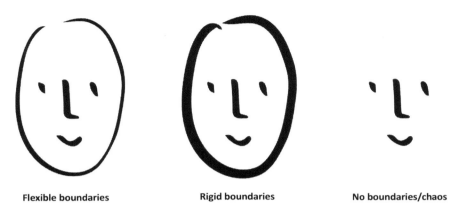

| Flexible boundaries | Rigid boundaries | No boundaries/chaos |

Figure 5.15

How do you do it?

- When we do not mentalize, it is normal for us to use one or more of the ways of thinking described on page 196.
- Are you flexible or rigid?
- How do you handle external challenges?
- Do you use teleological stance, where you feel the need to act and do something?
- Do you use psychic equivalence, where you convince yourself that "my version of reality is the right version"?
- Do you use pretend mode, where you detach mental states from reality?
- Try to think of examples where you found yourself using the teleological stance, psychic equivalence, or pretend mode. What happened in the situation? What were you thinking, and how did you feel? What brought you out of that state of mind and back to a more mentalizing way of thinking? The mere fact that you reflect on the reason for your actions is a form of mentalization. This is the best way to exercise and develop your ability to mentalize.

Chapter 6

Challenges in parenting

We began this book by admitting that being parents is not always easy. Chapter 6 deals with some of the specific challenges that you might face when bringing up children and attempts to outline what constitutes good parenting, such as playing with your child, the importance of physical touch, having serious conversations with your child, and encouraging mentalization between siblings and between different groups of parents. Turn to this chapter for help if you find yourself in a dilemma or if you are looking for ways to handle recurring challenges in parenting. We have attempted to apply the models we have used throughout the book. Furthermore, we refer to mentalization theory as well as research on child development.

The beginning of Chapter 6 suggests ways for you to create a good environment around and with your child. In particular, this chapter deals with common themes that tend to present a challenge to parents, such as shame and guilt in parenting, having serious conversations with your children, sibling rivalry, child sexuality, conflicts, boundaries, and lying. The remainder of the chapter deals with more serious topics such as grief, alcohol, trauma, and bullying, which are all things that parents must deal with but which are hopefully not a part of the family's everyday life for any long period of time.

The chapter – and, by extension, the book – concludes with a section called "The empty nest." At one point, the child will leave the nest and the parents face a new challenge of being a safe harbour for the child to return to for security, whilst at the same time making a new life for themselves without the child.

Play

"In play, a child is always above his average age," says the child psychologist, Lev Vygotsky (1962). That is, in play, the child is able to do things that it has not fully learned yet. From birth, the child is ready to play with adults. For the child, play opens up a gateway for learning and developing new skills. For instance, through play, the child can learn to express emotions, learn about the surrounding world, develop physical and motor skills, explore other perspectives, and practice ways to handle difficult experiences.

Play is a breeding ground for experimenting with emotions and skills that are not yet fully developed. This must be supported, even protected. The good thing about play is that it is joyful and intrinsically motivated – exactly because "it's only playing" (Winnicott 1971). Play is also of great importance when it comes to developing the capacity for mentalization because it allows the child to learn about itself and others. Similarly, role playing games are a way for the child to experiment with being in another person's mind and experience mental states that are not its own (I am the baby, and I'm hungry).

Suggestions and strategies

Some parents find it hard to engage in play with their children, perhaps because their own parents did not play with them when they were young. Remember that the child has no expectations of you as a parent – it is just a bonus to be able to share this moment with the child and enjoy it. In order for children to be able to immerse themselves in play, they need to feel safe and secure.

Example

On Christmas Day, a father and his son unwrap a huge box of Legos featuring a city centre. The father thinks that "this is going to be great" and that it is a good opportunity for him and his son to talk about the function of a city and its role in people's lives. The father finds the instructions and starts dividing the various pieces into piles. The boy is assembling a tower block, and he has incorporated a twig from a Christmas decoration and a piece of kitchen roll into the landscape around the building. The father is about to stop the boy and tell him that there should only be Lego bricks in the city, but he catches himself because he can see that his son is having fun mixing other things with the bricks. The father follows his son's example and takes some elves off a Christmas landscape and puts them in the city landscape. The boy looks up and grins, and they start chatting about their project.

MODEL **PLAY**

Figure 6.1

How do you do it?

- Play with your children every day. You do not have to do it for long; the important thing is that you do it.
- Make time for child-directed play.
- Join in when a playful situation arises.
- Help yourself take playing seriously by remembering that play has intrinsic value and that children learn a lot when they play. By playing with your children, you show them that their world is important.
- Do not let your own ambitions interrupt the game – children's play does not always conform to your own visions.
- Do not confine yourselves to organized play with toys. You can also play peekaboo, romping games, games with sounds, ball games, drawing on each other's backs, cuddles, blowing soap bubbles at each other, hide and seek, memory games, ruff and tumble play etc.

Physical contact and hugs

The importance of hugs and physical contact for children should not be under-estimated. In the mid-1940s, psychoanalyst Rene Spitz (1945) found that touch is necessary for children's survival. His research showed that a lack of physical contact resulted in developmental disorders and a higher mortality rate in children, even though their basic needs such as food and drink were fulfilled.

On the psychological level, touch makes the child feel important, loved, and protected. Physical contact and hugs are more than just a passing touch – they make a deep impression in our body and in our brain and make us feel connected to each other (Foghsgaard 2016). Our skin has sensory receptors which register even the smallest touch and sends signals to the brain, which then releases oxytocin (also known as the "love" or "cuddle" hormone). This hormone is released when we hug each other, hold hands, or have skin-to-skin contact. Oxytocin has various functions: it strengthens our immune system, relieves pain, reduces stress by lowering cortisol levels, and slows down the heart rate, thereby lowering blood pressure. The effect of oxytocin depends on the circumstances. Accidental touches on the bus have a lower effect than touches between people who know each other or are related. In the latter cases, physical touch strengthens the relation.

Following the intensified focus on sexual abuse, some fathers are afraid to touch their daughters, which is a pity. When it comes to physical contact with one's children, all adults need to use their common sense, respect boundaries, and have an understanding of the child's development, but when these things are respected, physical contact has a positive effect on the interaction between parent and child. After a conflict, a hug can be a good way to repair the relation and calm the child.

Suggestions and strategies

Teenagers are often not very interested in physical contact with their parents. One way to be allowed to give your teenager some love hormone might be through romping about with them or offering to rub their back or their feet.

Example

Jamie is a tall teenager, well over 6 feet, who does not care to be touched by his mother or his father. Sometimes, however, after a rough day at the soccer court, he likes to get a foot massage, which often turns out to be a relaxing and cosy way for them to spend time together.

MODEL PHYSICAL CONTACT AND HUGS

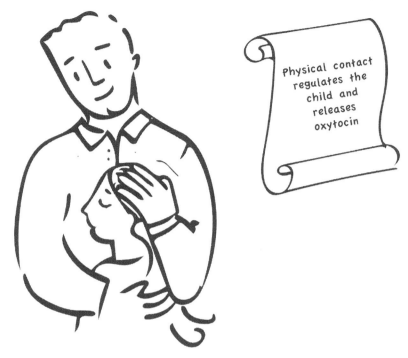

Physical contact regulates the child and releases oxytocin

Figure 6.2

How do you do it?

When small children experience intense emotions, physical contact at eye level can have a reassuring effect on the child: "Come and sit with Mom," "Let's go get your blanket, then we can sit together and talk about what made you so angry." So, it is advisable to:

- Have physical contact with your child from infancy.
- Gently place your hand on the child's shoulder if it is restless.
- Give the child a good hug when it feels natural to do so.

Ideas for working physical contact into your daily life

- Tumble, roughhouse, and play with your child.
- Rub your child's body and feet.
- Draw an image with your finger on the child's back – the child then has to guess what you have drawn.
- Hand-stacking game.
- Finding birthmarks.
- Gently pulling each of the child's fingers.

Conversations with children

The first conversations you have with your child are non-verbal, and this type of conversation continues to be important. Even with older kids, non-verbal signals are important. For example, you show your child that you want to talk to them through your tone of voice, eye contact, and language. When having conversations with children, all the points from Chapter 2 about the nautical universe are important – especially the point about keeping an open mind as well as choosing the right time and the right approach (p. 62).

Figure 6.3 lists a few things to keep in mind when you talk with your child. We focus on a conversation technique called useful monologues, where you mirror the child's emotions by telling stories about your own experiences as a child or about other children or young people (Egelund 1998; Andersen & Holter 1997). For instance, if your preschool child is worried about spending the night outside the home, you might tell them a story from your own childhood: "When I was a little girl, I used to worry about wetting the bed when I stayed over at a friend's house."

You can look for inspiration for the useful monologues in the emotional compass. It is a good idea to use anger, happiness, fear, and sadness as poles for the emotions you mirror. This enables the child to recognize as well as generalize the emotions. It is important not to have a predefined idea about the child's emotions and experiences but to give the child time and space to figure out its own experience. It is possible that the child experiences the situation differently from what you might think (Egelund 1998).

If you want to motivate the child to behave a certain way, it can be a good idea to pay attention to when the child expresses a desire for change on its own: "I think math is really hard, I'd like to practice more," "I wish I could learn to control my temper." Such statements are important because we are more influenced by what we say and argue ourselves than what we are told by others (Rollnick & Fabring 2016).

Suggestions and strategies

During conversations where you are doing something else at the same time, such as driving, you do not activate each other's mirror neurons. As a consequence, it can lead to some very good conversations.

Example

Jane is the mother of a teenage son and worries that he has started smoking. One day, as she and her son are in the car together, she talks about her Uncle Peter, who started smoking as a teenager. He would always smell of tobacco and sneak out for a smoke at least once every hour, so she could not understand why his parents did not notice. Jane goes on to talk about how Peter was the kind of person who had a hard time stopping once he had had one drag of a cigarette, but that people are different when it comes to addiction. Her son tells her that he has smoked a cigarette once, but that his friend did not even want to try it. He says that he has been offered to smoke several times since then, but that he has declined, because he does not want to smell of tobacco. Jane says that she is proud of him.

MODEL **CONVERSATIONS WITH CHILDREN**

Figure 6.3

How do you do it?

Adapt the conversation to fit the child's:

- Point of entry (see p. 62).
- Window of tolerance (see p. 59).
- Initiative and attention span.
- Current situation.
- Age and developmental level.
- Experience of being safe and secure.
- Linguistic ability.
- Chance to have time to express themselves.
- Desire and need for conversation – some children are wordy, while others are quiet. Respect your child. Gender roles can play a part here.

Suggestions for the conversation

- Create a rhythm for the conversation.
- Ask open questions.
- Many descriptions and few questions lead to better conversations.
- Show that you are listening – for instance by repeating what was said.
- It is a good idea to add something that is relevant and useful for the child.
- Use "useful monologues."
- If your child says something that shocks you, remember that this is a unique opportunity to be regulated, accountable, and mentalizing. Avoid catastrophizing the conversation; stay nuanced.
- Statements about what is right or wrong do not encourage dialogue and must be meted out in small measures. It can only be hoped that, sometimes, the child takes its parents' position on a subject to heart.
- Notice when the child expresses a desire for change.

Mentalization in groups of parents and children

It is an ongoing challenge to teach children how to be a part of social groups, understand hierarchies, and respect other people's attitudes, even when they do not agree with them. Fortunately, parents can encourage this by acting as role models for mentalizing behaviour – that is, by being regulated, accountable, and mentalizing.

There is a greater risk of mentalization failure in groups of children, and it can, at worst, continue in the parent groups. For example, two kids who quarrel over a toy or classmates who divide into two opposing groups might result in parents who refuse to greet each other.

As parents, there are two ways to stimulate a mentalizing environment among groups of children: firstly, by teaching your child mentalizing behaviour and encourage your child to be curious about other people's mental states and how they are manifested in behaviour, and secondly, by stimulating mentalizing behaviour in other parents. When you meet the other parents at parents' meetings, children's birthdays, or when picking up your child after a playdate, you can bring attention to the mentalizing environment among the children.

Suggestions and strategies

The adults must always be the mature ones and take responsibility for mentalization failures. The first person to notice a mentalization failure is obligated to bring mentalization back to the interaction.

Example

Ava and Emily's mothers are talking on the phone, deciding who should pick up the girls after the party they are going to this weekend. Emily's mother says: "I'm worried people will be smoking marijuana at the party." Ava's mother answers: "Yeah, I'm considering planting my own weed so that I can at least make sure they smoke something of quality." Emily's mother's immediate reaction is to tell her husband and anyone who cares to listen how inappropriate and stupid she finds Ava's mother. But instead, she listens so her and explains why she does not think it is okay for girls in the ninth grade to smoke marijuana.

Just then, Emily barges into the room, throws her bag in the corner, and complains: "My teacher is so stupid. He asked me to write a paper on modern ploughs. Such a ridiculous topic that no one can possibly find interesting, and now he has returned it to me with a bad grade. He is so stupid. I don't want to go to his classes anymore. Mom, can't you make a complaint to the school about him?"

Emily's mother listens patiently and asks her why she thinks the teacher chose that topic. In the end, Emily explains on her own that it is probably because they are doing a project week about agriculture at school. Emily's mother listens, and when Emily is more regulated, she says that it is important that we learn a little about our origins.

MODEL **MENTALIZATION IN GROUPS OF PARENTS AND CHILDREN**

Figure 6.4

How do you do it?

- Lead the way as a positive role model – be regulated, accountable, and mentalizing.
- Encourage your child to be flexible and look beyond behaviour. Support mentalization in your child.
- Talk about situations and experiences and help the child put into words its thoughts and hypotheses about other people's mental states.
- Support your child in serving as a positive role model who shows the other children how to mentalize.
- Be mentalizing towards the other parents. Talk to them instead of making fixed hypotheses about what is going on in their minds.
- Use your role as a parent to influence the children in your child's group through the other parents. Encourage them to see other perspectives and consider why other people act a certain way.

Sleep

Sleep is necessary for the child's as well as the teenager's development. If the body does not get the rest it needs during the night, it does not function well during the day. In order to fall asleep, the child must return to its safe harbour with its parents. For older children, it can be enough to know that the safe harbour is there if needed, but most young children need to have a mentalizing moment with their parents before they go to sleep.

When it comes to sleep, it is important to have boundaries and habits, such as a fixed bedtime and wake up time, to avoid excitable activities and instead focus on quieter activities, and to establish bedtime rituals. Children's sleep patterns depend on their age. Babies often need physical touch and massage to fall asleep. Small children benefit from routines that make them feel safe, as well as having something to take to bed with them, such as a teddy bear or a safety blanket. It is a good idea to make time for reading stories for little children who are not yet able to regulate themselves physically, because it helps them settle down and fall asleep.

For older children, you help them settle down by avoiding sugar and exciting stimuli as well as limiting screen time before bed. During adolescence, the body is developing at a rapid pace, and as a result, teenagers need a lot of sleep, and they often experience a shift to a later sleep-wake cycle, which means that they stay up late and rise late.

It is common for children and teenagers to sleep uneasily or to experience a disrupted sleep cycle periodically, where they feel restless and have a hard time falling asleep. We all have different sleep cycles, and no one – neither adults nor children – "sleeps through" every night without interruptions or awakenings. However, it is important to take troubled sleep and sleep disorders seriously and try out different strategies.

Suggestions and strategies

It is important for children that any relational disturbances or disagreements that have arisen during the day are repaired before they can settle down to sleep. Anxiety, anger, and conflicts in relation to friends, parents, or siblings must be carefully unravelled. Parents can serve as positive role models of the biblical saying: "don't let the sun go down on your anger."

Example

Marianne is a single mother of three children, and bedtime has become a complete chaos. Her teenage daughter Bella wants to listen to music, but it is also the unique time of day where she wants to talk to her mother. Three-year-old Isaac wants Marianne to lay down beside her until she falls asleep. If 9-year-old Mason does not go to bed at a certain time, he becomes overtired and makes a racket in the living room. In an attempt to be proactive, Marianne sits down with her kids to make agreements about bedtimes, bedtime rituals, and routines. This way, she is able to be there for all the kids before they go to sleep.

MODEL **SLEEP**

Figure 6.5

How do you encourage basic sleep hygiene?

- Stay within your child's reach when it is going to sleep.
- Encourage a good sleep cycle: Going to bed at the same time and rising at the same time regardless of the amount of sleep.
- Prepare your child: In 10 minutes you have to go brush your teeth, and then it is time for bed.
- Avoid any activities that rouse the child before bedtime, such as screens (television, computers, phones).
- Establish bedtime rituals and routines.
- Repair any conflicts that have arisen during the day.
- Talk about or write down any worries or anxieties well before bedtime.

How do you handle troubled sleeping?

- Listen to gentle music such as MusiCure or use apps that have exercises to help you fall asleep.
- Take a nice, long bath before bedtime.
- Use massage or do relaxation exercises.
- Yawn (it actually works) or count backwards from 1,000.
- Drink a cup of warm milk with honey before bedtime.
- Listen to relaxation exercises recorded by a primary caregiver.
- Do breathing exercises (breathe in, hold your breath whilst counting to six, exhale whilst counting to seven).
- Help yourself by thinking reassuring thoughts: "It is perfectly normal to have trouble sleeping sometimes."
- If necessary, get a ball blanket.

Sexuality

Children are born with sexuality (Fonagy 2008). As with everything else, development of sexuality is a result of interaction between environment and inherent biological development potential. The child's sexual experiences differ from other experiences such as emotional states in that their parents' task is not to mirror these experiences but rather to allow the child to discover and explore sexual sensations without feeling ashamed or that something is wrong with them. As parents, our job is to show the child that it is okay that it has a sexuality, but that there are certain rules about how to express sexuality in our culture, such as: "You should not touch your private parts in the living room. That is something you do when you are alone in your room."

The small child slowly discovers its own body and what feels pleasurable, and it is normal that the child explores its own genitals. Around age 2, the child becomes interested in differences between the sexes: who has penises and who has vaginas. From age 3 onwards, the child becomes interested in sexual games and may also enjoy trying out dirty words.

The child's first experiences with love might centre around its mother or father or a caregiver. Around age 9, the child may fall intensely in love with a popstar and later with a schoolteacher or a sports coach. None of these feelings are meant to be acted out. They are merely the first instances of the child's experimenting with the intense emotions connected with love and sexuality.

Teenagers are much more explorative about their own sexuality and desires. In fact, it is not until the teenage years that you begin to understand sexual feelings as expressions of sexuality. Similarly, it is not until the teenage years that you actually experience being part of a relationship in which your sexual feelings are recognized and mirrored in another. This is one of the few areas where parents cannot and should not attempt to mirror their child's feelings. In Denmark, the average age of sexual debut has remained at about 16 for many years and in the US 17 years of age (CDC.gov 2016). On the individual level, however, these numbers vary widely.

Suggestions and strategies

Children quickly discover that they can use the internet to find information about sexuality. It is a good idea to talk to them about it and tell them that what they are seeing on the internet is not reality. Sex on the internet is rarely a representation of what goes on in normal, loving relationships, and normal bodies do not look like the naked bodies you see online.

Example

Nine-year-old Madison has seen some pictures on Instagram of some women in a bubble bath. She takes a sexualized picture of herself in a bubble bath and puts it on her own Instagram account. Her mother asks her openly why she has uploaded the picture and gently tells Madison that she understands why she wanted to take a picture of herself in a bubble bath. She also tells her, however, that such a picture can be interpreted very differently by adults, and that there are some adults who think grown-up thoughts about children. In the end, they agree that Madison should delete the picture.

MODEL **SEXUALITY**

Figure 6.6

How do you support the child's normal sexual development?

- Do not shame the child about sexuality.
- Let your child know what is socially and culturally acceptable – for instance, that you touch yourself (masturbation) when you are alone in your room.
- Answer the child's questions about sexuality openly and honestly.
- Pay attention to the child's boundaries when you talk about sexuality. By respecting the child's boundaries, you let your child know that it has a right to have boundaries in sexual relationships.
- It is normal for children to be interested in what their own and other people's bodies look like and function. Children play sexual games, but these games have nothing to do with adult sexuality.
- It is normal that the child does not know where, what, and how you should touch other children and adults – and as a parent, it is your job to tell them.

How do you protect your child from abuse?

- The child needs to know the proper names for genitals and have age-appropriate knowledge about sexuality. This enables them to express it if someone touches it or violates its boundaries.

- Guidelines for children's sexual games:
    - The age difference between the children should not be more than two years.
    - The games must be age-appropriate. For example, small children should not act out adult sexuality.
    - Find out whether the child has been asked to keep some games secret.
    - Has the child been forced? Does the child appear scared or cowed?
    - Do the sexual games involve rituals or something that hurts?
- The child needs to know that it is always safe to tell its parents if it experiences something it does not understand or that makes it feel uncomfortable.
- The child needs to know that it should object if adults or older children touch its genitals.
- If you suspect that it is possible the child has been sexually abused, stay calm. If the parents are able to remain calm and mentalizing, the child might only experience symptoms and delayed reactions to a limited degree, or even not at all (Ensink et al. 2016).
- Children who have a good understanding of themselves and their right to boundaries are well protected against abuse.

Shame and guilt in parenting

After its first birthday, the child develops the ability to feel shame. When the child feels ashamed, it is expressed physically – the child looks down, hangs its head, or covers its face with its hands. Presumably, the child develops the ability to feel shame because shame is an emotion that regulates the child, who, at this age, is able to move around on its own and whose behaviour is impulsive and explorative. Shame might function as a break (developed through evolution) that helps the child control impulses and regulate needs (Shore 2003). The child's ability to feel shame, then, is a form of protection.

Shame also plays a part in the child's development in relation to social norms, and it is necessary for the child's healthy development to have experiences where it feels shame in a small scale. Shame is a part of the child's healthy development, and through interactions with its parents, the child develops guilt, which is more appropriate, since it is related to what the child has done and not a "physical break" related to the entire self. Guilt is more favourable than shame, because shame is more harmful to the self. Shame is thus directed towards yourself and who you are, and it can lead the child to hide away and isolate itself from its relations. Guilt, on the other hand, is directed towards behaviour, and its function is to make the child change its bad behaviour and apologize (Tangney et al. 2007). You can easily make someone feel ashamed through other means than words. Your tone of voice or your attitude can also make the child feel as if it is the child as a person who is wrong.

Pride is the "greater cousin" of shame and guilt. Children need to be praised in order to feel that they have social value. Therefore, pride encourages good behaviour and positive self-esteem.

Suggestions and strategies

Parents should be aware that children who grow up in shame-inducing environments easily feel threatened and detached from their parents. Such children are more likely to adapt themselves to their surroundings, feel ashamed of themselves, and take responsibility for the destructive family environment. Shame and submission might function as a way for the child to survive when it is impossible to fight, flee, or freeze. Often, shame helps the child make sense of something meaningless – it is better to be a devil in a world controlled by God than to live in Hell (Finkelhor et al. 1983).

Example

Two-and-a-half-year-old Sally pulls the tail of the family cat, and her mother tells her: "Sally, don't pull its tail; you should pet it instead." Sally moves to stand in the corner with her head bent. Her mother has never seen her react this way before, and Sally's reaction startles her. She hurries to comfort her daughter, hugs her close, and tells her: "Come, we'll pet the cat together."

Afterwards, she worries about why Sally had such a strong reaction to her reproach, until her friend explains to her that at this age, Sally is instinctively developing the ability to feel shame. Now, the mother's job is to help Sally regulate her feelings of shame and transform it into guilt, pride, and mastery.

MODEL **SHAME AND GUILT IN PARENTING**

Shame	Guilt
Directed at core self – change is impossible	Directed at behaviour – changing behaviour is possible
Isolation	Apologizing
Protecting the self, distancing and separating oneself from others	Encourages the ability to create social bonds
Related to anger	Related to empathy
Increases stress hormones: cortisol and proinflammatory cytokines	No increase of stress hormones
Directed towards oneself	Directed towards oneself as well as another
Teenagers who have grown up in a highly shame-inducing environment are more likely to commit violence and crime and are at a greater risk of exhibiting suicidal behaviour.	Teenagers who have learned to transform shame into guilt are more likely to engage in volunteer work and positive activities in their community.

Shame   Guilt

Figure 6.7

Source: Tangney et al. 2007

How do you do it?

- It is important that parents do not induce shame in their children, because it will make the child feel insecure about its own emotions as well as its relationship with its parents (Cooper & Redfern 2015).
- Parents encourage the child's journey from shame to guilt by explaining that there is something wrong with the child's behaviour – not the child itself.
- It is better for the child if parents encourage pride and good social behaviour in their child rather than shame.
- When parents recognize feelings of shame in their child and make sure to re-establish the relationship after a conflict, they encourage the child's ability to cope and transform shame into guilt.

- Parents must be able to balance their feelings of guilt, that is, to take the appropriate amount of responsibility for their actions and be able to apologize.
- It is important to be able to regulate shame and guilt in a way that is appropriate for the child's current level of development. It is hard for small children to regulate their emotions, and as a result, they can feel overwhelmed by feelings of shame.
- Teenagers are very vulnerable to feelings of shame. Small children think in a very concrete way, but teenagers are better at mentalization and understanding complex emotions and relationships as well as how their own behaviour influences these things.

Siblings

The first social context in which the children can experiment with social relations is in relation to their siblings. Children can support, isolate, tease, and learn from each other. In the sibling relationship, children learn to negotiate, cooperate, and compete. They learn to make friends and allies and to gain prestige. They learn to decode and understand social hierarchies and to achieve recognition for their skills. Siblings also provide the child with a great opportunity to practice mentalization. Siblings know each other's inner worlds very well and know what hurts each other the most, so they constantly use this information to test their theories about the other sibling's mind by teasing them. As parents, it can sometimes be difficult to remember all the positive areas of learning that are available in the sibling relationship. A study has shown that siblings aged 2–4 had six fights an hour on average (Forster 2014).

The experiences that children gain in their relationships with their siblings have a great influence on their life. They bring these experiences with them in their interactions with peers and in the world outside the family. Here, they will often follow the same social guidelines that were established in their relationship with their siblings. Outside the family, the child will also gain new experiences with social relations which they can bring back to their sibling relationship. This process is not always unproblematic, for instance when the younger sister learns that she also has a right to be in charge. Later, as they grow up and bring these experiences into their adult lives, it is important that the parents have paid attention to the different positions the children have taken in the sibling relationship. These positions can greatly affect the way they handle social relationships as adults.

Siblings are the only ones who have experienced their family from the inside. As a result, they have a unique opportunity to reflect together on the environment that has influenced them and made them who they are. As parents, you can create an environment that encourages siblings to talk about and reflect on their family – and to be critical. In this way, you give your children a gift they can benefit from throughout their lives.

Suggestions and strategies

The best way for parents to support a healthy sibling relationship is by encouraging their children to have fun together (Siegel & Bryson 2012). Create joyful moments and experiences for your children to have together. The greatest danger to a sibling relationship is not conflicts but rather when siblings ignore each other and do not care about each other.

Example

Two sisters are having a fight. It escalates, and the older sister, Riley, tells her younger sister: "You are really bad in school." The younger sister, Hazel, retorts: "And it is true what you have been writing in your diary, you *have* become too fat!" In a second, they have hit each other's sore spots. Their father is sitting comfortably in the sofa, considering whether he should intervene, until he hears his eldest daughter slamming the door to her room. A short while later, Hazel tentatively knocks on Riley's door and asks her if they should watch an eyebrow tutorial on YouTube together. Riley lets her in, and after a few minutes they emerge together to get some healthy snacks because they are going to watch a movie together.

MODEL **SIBLINGS**

Figure 6.8

How do you do it?

- A close relationship between siblings will inevitably involve challenges and conflicts and offers many opportunities for learning about relationships, conflicts, and mentalization.
- It is important to accept that conflicts are a natural part of any close social relationship between people who know each other well.
- Allow siblings to resolve conflicts on their own, when they are able to.
- Focus on situations where siblings are in agreement and cooperate.
- If you need to intervene, remember to look beyond the conflict and consider both perspectives.
- If possible, it is preferable if the siblings can come together to agree on a solution.
- Some situations require a "Solomonic solution" – that is, a compromise by means of something external that can divide the resources fairly (e.g. a chalkboard, or a sign up form to put one´s name on).
- In conflicts, use the "mentalization toolbox."
- Parents easily fall into the trap of treating their children differently based on their understanding of each child. Notice if you tend to regard one as a victim and the other as the trouble maker, then break your pattern.
- Make time to give each child special attention.
- Encourage a healthy sibling relationship by creating joyful moments and experiences.

Lies

When people discover that they have been lied to, it evokes intense emotions such as anger, anxiety, shame, and hurt. More often than not, this results in mentalization failure and thus a lack of understanding of the child and why it is lying. These failures can be lengthy, making it hard to return to a mentalizing approach to the child. Usually, children do not lie more than other people. However, there are certain stages of child development where they tend to lie more – such as around age 4 and again in their teenage years, where 98% admit that they lie once in a while (Elvén & Wiman 2016).

Children who have experienced trauma and neglect are more likely to lie than other children, chiefly due to low self-esteem and delayed reactions to the trauma. These children are even more in need of mentalizing interaction than other children, so if you encounter a vulnerable child who tells lies, encourage your own child to include this child, who is otherwise likely to be further excluded because of its lies (for more on this subject, see Hagelquist & Skov 2014).

When you encounter lies in children, it is important to understand what lies are and how to handle different lies (Feldman 2007). Lies tells us something about the mental state of the liar and should therefore be approached with curiosity and a wish to understand the liar's mental state – especially, to understand the intention behind the lie – as well as the mental state of the one who has been lied to. There are four different types of lies: white lies, cosmetic lies, deliberate lies, and cover stories. The model on page 226 can be used to determine which type of lie you have been told and to get ideas for how the lie can be addressed.

Suggestions and strategies

Deliberate lies are the rarest type of lie. Therefore, you should be extra careful with thoughts such as: "She is lying to me deliberately to hurt me." If it is really a case of deliberate lies, you should always intervene against them, as there will be fewer of such lies if you respond to them. Remember, however, that they are fairly common around age 3–5 and in the teenage years. When it comes to working with deliberate lies, it is just as important that adults lead the way in creating a family culture in which everyone knows that deliberate lies are inappropriate and socially unacceptable, in adults as well as children.

Example

Fifteen-year-old Olivia has started drinking alcohol. Her mother found out that Olivia has bought a bottle of vodka and hid it in her closet under some clothes. She pours the vodka down the drain, replaces it with water, and has a bit of fun noticing how Olivia brings some vodka with her whenever she goes to a party with her friends. When the bottle of vodka is empty, Olivia is convinced that she has a very high tolerance for vodka. At the next party, she drinks a lot of it and gets so drunk that her mother is called to come pick her up. The mother has learned that it is not a good idea for adults to lie and deceive.

MODEL LIES

Child development and lies

The 3–5-year-old child has just learned that others do not always know the same things that they do. This enables them to lie, and it is a great step in terms of development.
Teenagers are more loyal to their friend group than to their parents. This is a natural part of breaking away from dependence on their parents and a sign that they need their own personal space. The result is that 98% of teenagers tell lies once in a while.

White lies

White lies mainly serve a social function and are not intended to hurt others or to be used for personal gain.
People tell white lies to conform to social norms, avoid awkward situations, support others, or to keep the conversation going.

Cosmetic lies

Cosmetic lies protect the person from feelings of inferiority. You lie to appear or feel better than you are.

How do I support my child when it lies?

When your child starts to tell lies, remember that it is a sign that it is developing and has acquired a mentalizing skill. In a gentle way, help the child understand that it is not okay to lie.
Accept that it is normal for teenagers to lie whilst also maintaining the view that lying is an inappropriate way to deal with difficult situations. Consider whether the boundaries in the home are too strict, leaving the young person no other choice but to lie.

What to work on

Help the child find other ways to express things that are difficult to say.
Teach the child that it is almost always better to tell the truth, but that there are social situations where it can be appropriate to tell a small white lie to avoid hurting someone else.

What to work on

Cosmetic lies are connected with low self-esteem. Children who tell cosmetic lies are vulnerable to criticism and punishment. The person who is most likely to be negatively affected by this type of lie is the liar himself.
Work on improving the child's low self-esteem, and gently talk to the child about the lie. You can tell about your own lies to normalize (remember when you yourself were a teenager you must have told a lie) and take the shame part out of the discussion.

Deliberate lies

The liar has a deliberate intention to deceive others to gain their trust, for personal gain, to avoid trouble, or to hurt other people.

What to work on

If the child is telling deliberate lies, parents should remember that there will be fewer lies when you react against them. Parents must lead the way in creating an environment where there is consensus that it is inappropriate and socially unacceptable for adults as well as children to tell such lies. The best way to repair a relationship after a deliberate lie has been told is for the liar to admit to their lie and to apologize.

Cover stories

Cover stories refer to lies told by people who have experienced severe neglect and/or trauma. These lies are not in keeping with reality, but they contain elements of reality and may involve intense, unprocessed emotions. They can be understood as the mind's way of coping with disconnected fragments of traumatic experiences.

What to work on

Remember that the child does not intend to lie.
Give the child a gentle reality check.
Remember that these stories are told by vulnerable, traumatized children.
Punishment and public humiliation are inadvisable.

Figure 6.9

Boundaries

The term boundaries is often mentioned in relation to parenting. Boundaries are all about teaching children what sort of behaviour is unacceptable in their family and culture. Parents need to set boundaries in order for the child to become a well-functioning member of its culture. Throughout life, people must use their ability to set boundaries for themselves and others. When parents are able to set boundaries for their child, they simultaneously teach the child how to set mature boundaries for others.

Children learn boundaries by looking to their parents' behaviour and the way they respond to the child's behaviour. The aspects of the child and the child's behaviour that parents choose to focus on, negatively as well as positively, are picked up on by the child, who will then attempt to stay within these limits. Therefore, it is a good idea to take time to consider which boundaries you think it is important for your child to learn, and which can be formulated through rules and guidelines, that are meaningful and easy to understand for the child. The child learns mature boundary-setting, by the parents talking to the child about expectations and the reasons behind the boundaries.

As a parent, you have come a long way if you are able to reason what boundaries should be applied in the family, but in reality you are not able to foresee everything. Luckily our emotions, specifically the emotion anger, help us to set boundaries, look after ourselves, and feel when something or someone have crossed our boundaries. Mentalizing, meaningful and easy to understand everyday age-appropriate routines, creates room for the child´s development process.

Suggestions and strategies

When setting boundaries for your child, think about its developmental level. Consider if you need to protect (here, we are outside the child's zone of development, and you need to set boundaries), support (an opportunity for learning in which our own flexibility as a parent and taking into account the unpredictability of life, can encourage the child to learn, with adult guidance), or grant autonomy (the young person makes their own decisions, and their boundaries must be respected).

The task of setting boundaries changes as the child grows older. Four- to 8-year-olds test the boundaries, but 9- to 12-year-olds are more outward-oriented. This period offers many opportunities for children to learn to set their own boundaries, but they need their parents to help them. In the teenage years, from age 13–18, boundaries usually revolve around the extent and content of the young person's social life, but it is also important to make space for autonomy.

Example

Fourteen-year-old Ethan is very interested in parkour. He has picked out two houses and wants to attempt to jump from one to the other. However, his parents forbid him to do it. They think the buildings are too high and that it is too dangerous. Ethan is furious. He says that his mother is stupid, his father old, and that both of them are boring. He continues to pester, beg, and threaten them to let him do it. At home he behaves like a trapped, angry dog and sets his face against everything his parents propose. He bullies his siblings and refuses to partake in meals or any other social activities in the family. His parents stand their ground but also have to endure his emotions.

MODEL **BOUNDARIES**

External regulation – regulated by others	Zone of proximal development – self-regulation with guidance	Internal regulation – Self-regulation
Is still unable to do it alone. The child needs to feel protected and needs someone to help it through.	Is almost able to do it alone but still needs support. The child needs attentiveness and involvement.	Is able to do it alone. The child's independence is respected.

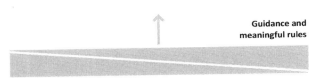

Guidance and meaningful rules

Setting boundaries

Figure 6.10

How do you do it?

- Boundaries and limits create overview and a calm atmosphere.
- It is easier to comply with rules and boundaries that you have been able to influence.

- Boundaries must be balanced so that they are neither too rigid nor too slack, resulting in chaos.
- As the child grows older, it is important that the boundaries are modified to fit the child's age.
- It is a good idea to be proactive and discuss rules and boundaries on family meetings. Inquire into the mental states that underlie not only the boundaries themselves but also any opposition against certain boundaries. Such family meetings greatly influence children's development of mentalization (Siegel & Hartzell 2003: 237).
- Consider boundaries and limits that are appropriate for the child's age. Boundaries determine what we do in the family and removes conflict issues from the concrete situation. The focus of the boundaries varies with the child's age:
  - Age 0–3: morning routines, routines surrounding mealtimes, routines for dropping off and picking up the child, sleeping rituals.
  - Age 3–5: morning routines, routines surrounding mealtimes, routines for dropping off and picking up the child, sleeping rituals, rules surrounding screen time and language.
  - Age 6–12: morning routines, duties, responsibilities, participating in the family, spare time, screen time, and homework.
  - Age 13–18: Homework, duties, responsibilities, curfews – participating in the family, and life outside the family.
- There might be reasons for relaxing the demands, but in general, children should experience that parents are true to their word. Children feel more secure when they know that their parents adhere to their decisions, and clear rules and boundaries give rise to fewer conflicts (Siegel 2013; Forster 2014).

Conflicts and the conflict staircase

The term conflict means "coming into collision." From the perspective of mentalization, conflicts happen when minds collide. As a child grows up, multiple conflicts are bound to arise between child and parents, between siblings, between parents and school, and not least between the child and its friends. Even though conflicts are sometimes unwelcome, they are a unique opportunity for children to learn that minds are different and that conflicts are a natural part of social interaction.

All conflicts hold the possibility for contact, development, and learning. If the parents are able to handle the conflict in such a way that by the end of the conflict, both parties feel heard and respected. In the relationship between parent and child there is no reason to avoid conflicts. When conflicts are handled in a mentalizing way, it leads to fewer conflicts – even when the conflicts end with a "no" to the child's request. It sounds easy, but it is not.

Conflicts are often portrayed as a staircase where you move either up or down depending on the intensity of the conflict (Glasl 1997). At the first level of the staircase, the conflict remains focused on the original issue from which it originated. At this level, mentalization failure can be avoided through dialogue. At the middle level, the conflicting parties are no longer able to talk, and both of them feel that they are in the right. Here, you seek support from others and attempt to form alliances, "her against us." At the last level, one's mental image of the other person has been erased and replaced with an enemy image: Mental strategies such as "I am the victim and the other person is evil," giving "the silent treatment," and spiteful remarks are used as weapons at this level. This phenomenon is also known as mental blindness, since your ability to mentalize the other person gradually disappears as the conflict escalates, which leads to a dehumanization of the other person (Baron-Cohen 1995).

In order to resolve the conflict, you must "move back down the staircase." That is, you must work against mental blindness, refrain from thinking about the other person as "the evil one," and avoid forming alliances, and instead you must try to talk to each other. In conflict resolution, parents are role models for their children.

Suggestions and strategies

Try to keep an open mind throughout the conflict. This may not come easy, and it is, in fact, almost unnatural to do so, since conflicts evoke intense emotions and therefore mentalization failure. The challenge is, however, to teach your child to see things from your perspective. You cannot expect your child to be able to do this if *you* have a hard time understanding their perspective and see them as spoiled, badly behaved, selfish, etc. Remember to repair the relationship after a conflict. If you have escalated the conflict, the best way to teach the child to apologize is by setting a good example.

Example

Eight-year-old Kayla and 10-year-old Aiden are siblings. There are having an argument about whose turn it is to play Fortnite. Kayla appeals to their older sister, 12-year-old Violet, who sides with Kayla. The argument develops into a screaming match. Aiden points out that Violet is using his computer, so he goes to her room to take it back. Kayla and Violet try to hold him back. Their mother, who has been following the spectacle, was hoping that the kids would de-escalate the conflict on their own. However, at this point they need someone with a more mature mind to intervene and mediate between them.

MODEL THE CONFLICT STAIRCASE

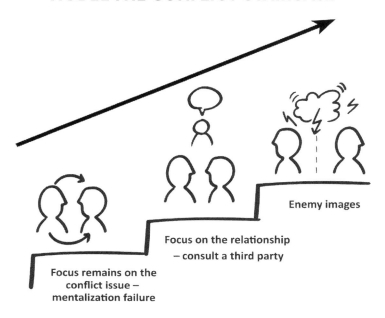

Figure 6.11

How can conflicts serve as learning opportunities?

- View conflicts as a possibility for your child to develop.
- Through conflicts, the child learns to tolerate and endure intense emotions.
- Try to keep an open mind in conflicts.
- Calm your own mind so that you can be a positive role model for your child and use the situation as a learning opportunity.
- In order to handle conflicts, you must create an environment that focuses on understanding the other person's perspective and clearing up misunderstandings.
- The goal is to maintain a close relationship even when you are going through a conflict.
- When siblings are conflicting at the lowest of the staircase, parents should let them resolve the conflict on their own. At the second level, they might need a grown-up to intervene. At the third level, the siblings should be separated until mentalization is re-established.
- When there is a conflict between the parents, it is important that they explain the process to their children. Let them see that conflicts are a natural part of a relationship and that it is possible to work through them.
- Remember to repair the relationship after a conflict.

Bullying – victim–offender–bystander

Parents always worry about their child being bullied – and with good reason, since it has many negative side effects. In general, bullying refers to an attempt to hurt another child and exclude them from the group.

According to the theory of mentalization, understanding a conflict as comprised by a cruel bully and a victim leads you to focus on individuals, placing the bully at the root of the problem. As a result, you focus your attention on the intention behind the bully's behaviour and draw conclusions about the reason why they feel the need to bully others (Twemlow et al. 2004).

However, by breaking the issue down to individual people, you ascribe the children certain roles and perspectives, fixing on a rigid assumption about the individual child's mental state. This is known as a victim–offender–bystander triangle. Imagine that Catherine is bullying Lyanna at school, making Lyanna the victim and Catherine the offender, and the rest of the class become bystanders.

Instead, looking at bullying as a case of groupwide mentalization failure allows you to look at bullying not as a problem between individuals but as a group phenomenon. Everyone must take responsibility for the bullying – bystander, victim, and offender alike. One needs to understand not only the mind of the bully but of the victim and the bystanders as well in order to dissolve the defective social patterns that the bully and the victim are symptomatic of. Taking a mentalizing approach to bullying means nuancing the positions and mentalize everyone involved. By taking a bird's-eye perspective on the situation, you look at bullying as a sign of deficient mentalization and relationship formation within a group. This enables you to re-establish the ability to mentalize with all members of the group.

Suggestions and strategies

Bullying is damaging to a child, and parents need to be attentive and act if they suspect that their child's class is developing an environment that allows for bullying. Contact the teacher, talk to the other parents, and remain the most mentalizing person. Even though it can be difficult, it is a great advantage to your child if you are able to remain mentalizing towards classmates, parents, and teachers. Help your child develop strategies to handle bullying.

Example

At a parent's evening for sixth grade, the parents express concern that Danny is always going after Laura. He says rude things to her, such as: "Where did you go on holiday? Oh, wait, your mom can't afford to go on holiday, because you're poor, right?" or "Your mom smokes so much, don't you think she'll die of cancer? Then you'll probably go to an orphanage, because you don't have a father, do you?"

The group of parents discuss these incidents, focusing on how Danny's behaviour is damaging the class as a whole. At one such meeting, however, the parents start to talk about ways to shift the fixed positions. The parents are asked to make an effort to invite Danny over more often. The children are asked to take collective responsibility and, instead of being bystanders, to react when they hear someone using insulting or abusive language – no matter who is using it. These initiatives change the class dynamic for the better.

MODEL THE VICTIM-OFFENDER-BYSTANDER TRIANGLE

Figure 6.12

How do you encourage a safe environment that prevents bullying?

- Work on the situation in the group in which the victim–offender–bystander dynamic is in play. By enabling the group to express these situations in words, the ability of the group as a whole to shape the behaviour of individual members is strengthened.
- Help the child understand that bystanders have a responsibility to intervene and emphasize the importance of maintaining mentalization.
- Support the child to step out of the role as bystander, to have the courage to intervene in situations where someone is being bullied, and to stop non-mentalizing behaviour.

What do you do if your child is bullied?

- When your child tells you about bullying, take it seriously. Use the gangway (p. 64) and avoid mentalizing the other person too quickly. Even though bullying has to do with group dynamics, your child needs you to listen to their perspective. However, if your child is to learn to manage relational challenges, you need to encourage them to show interest in other perspectives.
- Teach your child strategies to avoid being bullied. Do not react to bullying – walk away. Seek help with friends or adults to avoid entering into the victim–offender–bystander triangle.

Alcohol

Alcohol is a part of many people's lives to a greater or lesser extent, but parents are often unsure about how to handle alcohol in relation to their adolescent child. It is important that parents consider ways to handle their child's consumption of alcohol. Here, we have included a questionnaire that is relevant in relation to parents' as well as teenagers' alcohol use.

In terms of parents' alcohol use, research has shown that adults on average wait 11 years before seeking help for their alcohol problems (Sundhedsstyrelsen 2015: 44). Most people who have experience with drinking alcohol know that alcohol affects your emotions – and naturally, it also affects mentalization. When parents feel stressed, alcohol can have a regulatory function, calming emotions and settling the nerves. Some parents' alcohol use means that they drink at night when the children are being put to bed, which keeps them from the children's important transition from being awake to sleeping. Children whose parents drink often feel that their worries about their parents' alcohol use are not taken seriously, and perhaps they even start to doubt their own emotions (Black 2001).

An alcohol addiction often develops gradually, as the frequency and quantity of alcohol slowly increases. Usually, people are able to maintain their ability to handle normal social situations – attending to children, home, and work – but as their consumption increases, they slowly lose the ability to see themselves from the outside. Most people are still able to do their job, but in other areas of their life things slowly start to fall apart, and the children and the partner have to compensate as the affected individual slowly loses their ability to register how much alcohol influences their life.

Suggestions and strategies

Test yourself using the following questionnaire. Seek help if your score is too high.

Example

Abigail's mother has a demanding job in management. After work, she has a glass or two of red wine to unwind and calm down. However, her use of alcohol makes her tired, and as a consequence it falls to 13-year-old Abigail to do the housekeeping and take care of the younger children. Often, the mother also needs Abigail to comfort her. One night, she sits at the edge of Abigail's bed, and says: "I've been thinking. You have been such a good girl, taking care of everything around here. Sweet

Abigail, it's taking too much of your energy. I'm sorry for that, and I hope you know that I really love you." Her mother's words fill Abigail with happiness. Finally, her mother has realized how much she is struggling and that her use of alcohol has turned into an addiction. Abigail has yearned to hear these words for years. Her mother continues: "Come on out of bed and let me hug you for a while, because of how much we love each other." Abigail realizes that her mother is drunk. The mother does not notice anything because the alcohol suspends her ability to see herself from the outside and Abigail from the inside.

MODEL **ALCOHOL**

AUDIT (Alcohol Use Disorders Identification Test)
A score of 8 or more suggests that the person has a problem with alcohol. A high score in the first three questions suggests an unhealthy level of drinking, a high score in questions 4–6 suggests addiction, whilst a high score in the rest of the questions suggests harmful and hazardous drinking.

Score	0	1	2	3	4
The first questions have to do with your recent drinking habits					
1 How often do you have a drink containing alcohol?	Never	Monthly or less	2–4 times a month	2–3 times a week	4 times a week or more
2 How many drinks containing alcohol do you have on a typical day when you are drinking?	1–2	3–4	5–6	7–9	10 or more
3 How often do you have six or more drinks on one occasion?	Never	Less than monthly	Monthly	Weekly	Daily or almost daily
The next five questions have to do with your drinking habits during the last year					
4 How often during the last year have you found that you were not able to stop drinking once you had started?	Never	Less than monthly	Monthly	Weekly	Daily or almost daily
5 How often during the last year have you failed to do what was normally expected of you because of drinking?	Never	Less than monthly	Monthly	Weekly	Daily or almost daily
6 How often during the last year have you needed a first drink in the morning to get yourself going after a heavy drinking session?	Never	Less than monthly	Monthly	Weekly	Daily or almost daily

AUDIT (Alcohol Use Disorders Identification Test)
A score of 8 or more suggests that the person has a problem with alcohol. A high score in the first three questions suggests an unhealthy level of drinking, a high score in questions 4–6 suggests addiction, whilst a high score in the rest of the questions suggests harmful and hazardous drinking.

	Score	0	1	2	3	4
7	How often during the last year have you had a feeling of guilt or remorse after drinking?	Never	Less than monthly	Monthly	Weekly	Daily or almost daily
8	How often during the last year have you been unable to remember what happened the night before because of your drinking?	Never	Less than monthly	Monthly	Weekly	Daily or almost daily

The last two questions have to do with your drinking habits during your life

9	Have you or someone else been injured because of your drinking?	No		Yes, but not in the last year	Yes, during the last year
10	Has a relative, friend, doctor, or other health care worker been concerned about your drinking or suggest you cut down?	No		Yes, but not in the last year	Yes, during the last year

Figure 6.13

Source: Simonsen & Møhl 2017: 257

How do you do it?

Parents and alcohol

- Calculate your score in the questionnaire. If your score suggests that you have a drinking problem, seek help. Lots of good support options and professional help are available.
- In the family, alcohol problems are often surrounded by secrecy. Have you told your children: "Don't tell anyone that . . ."?

- Ask your children about their thoughts on alcohol: "What have you noticed?"
- Notice if your children are overly focused on your alcohol consumption.
- Pay attention to any role reversals in the family. Does the child sometimes have to assume the parental role?
- Remember that it is not the person who drinks who is the problem. It is the alcohol that is causing the trouble, so remember to separate the person from his/her alcohol consumption.

Adolescents and alcohol

- Make sure that the young person knows about the health risks of alcohol consumption.
- Talk about alcohol – even if the young person is not drinking (they might start sooner than you would like) and when they start drinking (perhaps more than you would like).
- Prohibit alcohol consumption for as long as possible. The young person might violate your rules, but at least they know where their parents stand.
- It is inadvisable that young people drink alcohol for the first time at home. This sends a signal that alcohol is a positive thing and a sign of adulthood.
- Make it clear that it is always okay to call you for help if they have been drinking – even if they are not allowed to drink.
- Emphasize the importance of taking care of each other and see each other safely home.

Trauma

Some children will experience a traumatic event such as witnessing violence, suffering sexual abuse, undergoing surgery, or being in a car accident. Trauma impacts the child's mind in a way that no other experience can. Children who have experienced trauma might come to believe that they must be crazy because they are experiencing post reactions. As a rule, post reactions are the mind's way of helping the child understand and come to terms with the experience.

In 1980, when the first diagnosis of PTSD was developed, people did not think that children could be traumatized because their behaviour did not necessarily show any signs of post reactions. They were thought to be impervious to trauma. Today, we know that children can be traumatized, and researchers keep finding new examples that confirms this – for example, in recent years, studies have shown that children who witness domestic violence also develop PTSD (Kilpatrick & Williams 1997).

According to the theory of mentalization, parents make the best trauma therapists. If the child's parents are able to handle the trauma in a constructive way and attend to the child's needs, it protects the child from developing post reactions to the trauma (Cohen et al. 2006; Friedman et al. 2007). As a parent, it can be hard and overwhelming if your child has been traumatized. You may forget everything you used to be able to do. For example, imagine a mother who is usually very good at consoling her son. However, when it emerges that the older boy next door has violated her son sexually, she becomes so upset that she sobs and cries and subsequently distances herself from her son, who is only 6 years old.

It is very important that parents to support their child through a trauma because children are actually more resilient to trauma than adults, provided that they receive support from their parents (Levine & Kline 2007).

Suggestions and strategies

Boys often feel ashamed of having post reactions to trauma. Therefore, it can be a good idea to tell them that these reactions are often seen in soldiers who return from war. To them, it seems cooler to be someone who has the same symptoms as a soldier than to be someone who has flashbacks because they were terrified of syringes at the hospital.

Example

One night, 13-year-old Luke is home alone as a thief enters the house. The thief is intoxicated and threatens Luke. After this incident, he starts to imagine that he hears someone opening the door, even though no one is there. He is afraid to be alone in the house, and he no longer wants to meet up with his friends – something he used to love to do. He is pessimistic and lies awake at night, unable to find rest. During this time, Luke's parents pay special attention to their son. They show him the trauma ostrich, which helps him understand that his reaction is completely normal and that it is his mind's way of coping with the traumatic experience.

MODEL **TRAUMA**

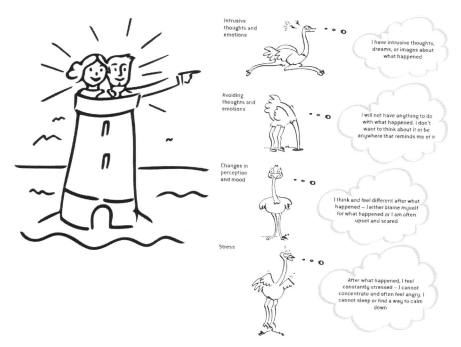

Intrusive
thoughts and
emotions

I have intrusive thoughts,
dreams, or images about
what happened

Avoiding
thoughts and
emotions

I will not have anything to do
with what happened. I don't
want to think about it or be
anywhere that reminds me of it

Changes in
perception
and mood

I think and feel different after what
happened – I either blame myself
for what happened or I am often
upset and scared

Stress

After what happened, I feel
constantly stressed – I cannot
concentrate and often feel angry. I
cannot sleep or find a way to calm
down

Figure 6.14

How do you do it?

- The adult needs to be the child's lighthouse who is regulated, accountable, and mentalizing.
- Restore everyday life – do everyday things: Rise at the usual time every morning, go to soccer practice, get homework done and enjoy the usual weekend treats. Re-establish the everyday rhythm helps normalise the situation.
- Parents can support the child by creating a coherent story about the traumatic situation. Show that you want to answer the child's questions and that it is okay for you to talk about it – even if it is difficult. Revisit the setting of the trauma and talk about what happened. Respect the child's boundaries when it needs a break.
- In cases of abuse, take care not to ask leading questions such as: "Did he do this and this?"
- Tell the child about post reactions to trauma, perhaps by referring to the trauma ostrich.
- Tell the child that some children think, feel, and do things that they did not think, feel, and do before the incidents, and that it is perfectly normal.

If the child does not spontaneously say anything, ask the child if it has felt that way. It is also a good idea to tell stories about other children or adolescents, who have been in similar situations, and reflect the emotions that your child may be feeling.

- If the child is showing avoidance coping behaviour, gently and gradually approach the things the child fears in a mentalizing way, by using assurances, gentle speech, or physical contact.

Divorce

For most people, divorce is a complex and difficult affair that brings about great changes. Despite the high divorce rates, every divorce is a heavy load to bear and a challenge for every child, family, and other affected parties. When parents are divorcing, it challenges the mentalizing environment surrounding the child. A divorce may involve intense emotions such as anger, jealousy, anxiety, sadness, and guilt, and intense emotions inhibit parents' ability to mentalize.

In addition, the need to mentalize with each other vanishes with the divorce. The person who leaves might even feel relieved that they no longer have to concern themselves with what is going on in the other person's mind. However, the children are caught between their two parents, and it remains the parents' job to create a mentalizing environment between mother and father – for the children's sake.

The conflicts and problems that existed between the parties in the relationship usually continue after the divorce. It may be surprising that the problems continue and maybe even worsen, and that you still have to address them together as co-parents. In some divorces, parents might be so preoccupied with their new relationship or their new life that they, for a time, are unable to mentalize in relation to their child. Falling in love has a negative effect on the ability to mentalize – perhaps because it has proven evolutionarily adaptive for humans to overlook their own emotions, needs, goals, and reasons, as well as those of other people, in order to improve their ability to make decisions (Fonagy 2008).

If it is hard to co-operate after a divorce, it is important that the parents make an effort to differentiate between their view of the other person as an ex-partner and as a co-parent. This can prove a very demanding task, but it is extremely important that parents are able to set aside their own needs and personal conflicts for the child's sake, and that they make a deliberate effort to put themselves in the child's place and do what is best for the child.

Suggestions and strategies

Make space for your child's perspectives and emotions, including the feelings of sorrow and loss the child may feel as a result of the divorce – even if it is hard for you to see and hear. Children's grief can last a long time and may return at later developmental stages.

Example

Eight-year-old Nathan's world falls apart when his father leaves his mother for another woman. No one can afford to stay in the house, and the family dog has to be put down. Nathan's mother is devastated, jealous, and angry. His father is happy and passionately in love. The father is frustrated with Nathan because he cries when he is put to bed at his father's new place. His father's girlfriend is convinced that Nathan's mother wants to ruin their new relationship by intensifying and sustaining his grief. The father wants Nathan to see a therapist, but Nathan refuses to go. At last, he admits that he is ashamed of being such a baby who cannot figure out how to be a big boy with divorced parents.

MODEL **DIVORCE**

Figure 6.15

How do you do it?

- Promise each other that you will do everything you can to work to together to be the best parents possible to your shared children. Remind yourselves and each other that a high level of conflict affects the child negatively and makes it more vulnerable.
- When communication goes awry, focus on the child and try to put yourselves in the child's place to better see what the child needs.
- Include the child in a way that allows the child to be heard. Only present the child with options that you are both able to live with.
- Avoid turning the child into a small adult who assumes their parents' worries and duties.
- Seek out others to confide in about the challenges of the break-up and your new life.
- Agree on a broad set of guidelines and norms for the child's two homes. This has a positive influence on the child's development and behaviour regulation (but accept that you are different people).

- Prioritize time and activities where the child's parents (preferably both at the same time) are present and available – preferably without the respective new families/partners.
- Support the child in getting outside help, and make sure that they have someone who is not emotionally involved to share their worries and thoughts with.
- Remember that the child may experience further losses due to the parents' new relationships. A new boyfriend or girlfriend and new stepchildren can evoke feelings of disappointment, anger, jealousy, and a sense of being set aside, which can greatly affect the child. In this case, it helps the child regulate its emotions if the parents take its feelings seriously.

Grief

Grief is a natural part of life. It is impossible to love and form close relationships without grieving when you lose them. Children also experience loss and grief. They might lose pets, grandparents, or, in some cases, parents or siblings.

Grief is a process that helps the child adjust to the loss. People used to think that you could get over a loss, but you will always have a connection to the one you have lost. A deceased person who has been a part of your life and your memories with that person – the good as well as the bad – will always be with you. The goal is not to get over the loss but to learn to live with it.

The child's age and personality as well as the family's resources, level of openness, and patterns of reaction are all important circumstances surrounding a loss. A child will experience loss differently depending on its development stage. The child can grieve over its grandfather in a new way when its brain is able to comprehend that the person who is gone will never come back. If the person who is lost is a parent or a sibling, the sense of loss will typically be activated on holidays – birthdays, Christmas, weddings, etc.

There is no right way to grieve. For children as well as adults, the best way to cope with a loss is to alternate between grieving and moving on. Today, grief is often viewed as an interaction between two tracks: processes of grief and processes of adjusting to the loss. These two tracks are equally important, and they work in parallel in the grieving person (Guldin 2014). Sometimes, members of a family or a relationship are divided into different tracks. In such cases, the task is to respect that both tracks are part of the healing process.

Parents often want to shield the children by keeping information from them, but when you experience something of immense significance, it is particularly important that children have confidence in the adults. The worst thing is if children start to lose their trust in the adults, because it makes them feel insecure and unsafe. If you, as a parent, are so overwhelmed with grief that you find yourself unable to talk to your child about the loss for a time, it is a good idea to ask other adults for support. Grown-ups who are going through a crisis often need practical support – remember to ask for help.

Suggestions and strategies

It is okay to show that you are grieving. It is a natural emotion, and as long as you signal to you child that "we will be all right," you also serve as a role model, showing you child how to mourn.

Example

At school, 8-year-old Caleb reacts with sadness, stomach ache, and trouble concentrating. At a parent–teacher consultation, it emerges that

Caleb's grandmother recently died after a very short illness. In fact, his mother has not told him yet, because she wanted to protect him. However, when she talks to Caleb about what has happened and they visit the grave together, he is able to trust her again and starts to get back to normal.

MODEL **GRIEF**

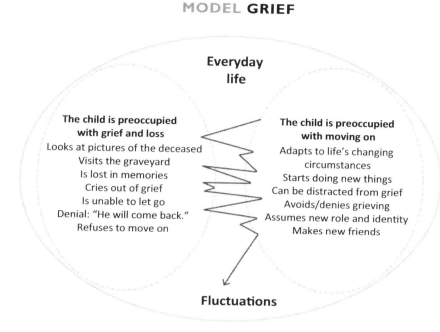

Figure 6.16

Source: Stroebe & Schut 1999

How do you do it?

- Be honest. Do not let the child lose its confidence in the adults.
- Talk about the loss – where, how, and why – in a way that is appropriate for the child's age.
- Funerals and other rituals surrounding death are important. They give concrete expression to the loss, and it has a healing effect to mourn together.
- Avoid overstimulation your child when talking about death and mourning. Pay attention to the child's signals.
- Acknowledge that sorrow can be experienced and expressed in many different ways.
- If the child is stuck in one of the tracks, gently push them in the other direction. If the child is preoccupied with the loss, you might need to help distract them from their grief through music or other activities. On the other hand, if the child never mentions the loss, it might be a good idea for

the adults to touch on the subject, talk about the deceased, show pictures, and take the child to see the grave.

- Have the courage to talk about the lost one when it feels natural.
- Answer your child's questions about death openly and honestly.
- Take care to talk about survivor's guilt, where you feel that you are not allowed to be happy because someone else has died.
- Talk to the child about how people react to grief and loss, so the child understands that there is nothing wrong with them. When you grieve, it is normal to miss the lost one and to feel lonely, abandoned, anxious, worried, sad, angry, relieved, guilty, and despairing.

The empty nest

When the child leaves the nest, it is like a great, beautiful ship setting out from the port, the parents standing proudly on the wharf and waving goodbye. However, more often than not the young person returns to "port" – bringing their laundry.

The age from 18–25 is an important stage in life, featuring new friendships, college, and learning to cope with adult life, but it is also a period where many things can go awry (substance abuse, bad friends, no education, and so on).

It is important to let one's children go gently and at a pace appropriate for the young person's level of development. Breaking away from the childhood home is the first time the young person experiences a radical change, and it is important that it is a good experience. The young person might return to their childhood home to stay a few times, perhaps due to break-ups, changing studies, or economic difficulties. As a parent, it can be challenging to make space for the young person and provide support on the one hand, and on the other hand to maintain the ideas and routines of your new life without your child. *The empty nest* refers to the sense of sadness, loss, and loneliness that parents might feel when their children leave the nest. It is important for you as well as your child how you handle this new chapter of your adult life (Mayo Clinic 2013).

Suggestions and strategies

When your children bring back their own children, you have graduated as a parent. You have been through the entire journey, while your child must learn everything from scratch. It is important that parents show their grown children that they have confidence in them. Be their lighthouse and remember how hard it was and how little you knew when you first became a parent. Allow your children to learn to master parenthood on their own, with you as their support system.

Example

It is a great change in John and Catelyn's life when their daughter leaves the nest. All of a sudden, the house is very quiet. There is no longer any reason for the structures that have shaped the family's everyday life for the past 20 years. Each of the parents try out new hobbies, and they attempt to reconnect anew as a couple rather than simply a team that takes care of the work and manages the household. As they are slowly getting used to this new balance, their daughter moves back home. She has quarrelled with her boyfriend and is unhappy with her courses at college. She moves back and forth another couple of times until she has finally settled down in her new life.

Years later, their daughter brings home their first grandchild. Catelyn thinks of herself as a fully qualified parent and wants to show her daughter how to mentalize with a baby. However, she controls herself and hands the reins over to her daughter, allowing her to develop her own parenting style.

MODEL THE EMPTY NEST

Figure 6.17

- Give your child space and acknowledge their autonomy and independence.
- Show your child that you have confidence in them and that you trust that they are able to handle the new challenges.
- Allow the child to return home several times – either to stay or just to get support.
- It is important that the child feels that they have the possibility to come home to let go of their responsibilities and regress a little – so expect the young person to become more childish again when they return home.
- Sometimes, it can be necessary for the parents to reach out to keep in touch with their child. During this time, the young person is focused on figuring out what he or she wants to do with their life, but they still have a "safety line" in their family and their parents, should they need them.
- Acknowledge the feelings of sadness that the empty nest may evoke.
- Reflect on the possibilities of this new stage of your life.
- Be a mentalizing grandparent.

References

Ainsworth, M. & Bell, S.M. (1970). Attachment, exploration, and separation – illustrated by the behavior of one-year-olds in a strange situation. *Child Development*, 41(1): 49–67.

Allen, J., Bleiberg, E. & Haslam-Hopwood, G. (2003). Mentalizing as a compass for treatment. *Bulletin of the Menninger Clinic*, 67.

Allen, J.G. & Fonagy, P. (2006). *Handbook of Mentalization-Based Treatment*. Chichester: Wiley & Sons.

Allen, J.G., Fonagy, P. & Bateman, A. (2010). *Mentalisering i klinisk praksis*. København: Hans Reitzels Forlag.

Andersen, T.K. & Holter, H. (1997). Jeg vil jo ikke kalle mamma en fyllik. *Fokus*, 2: 124–134.

Asen, E. & Fonagy, P. (2011). Mentalization-based therapeutic interventions for families. *Journal of Family Therapy*, 34(4): 347–370.

Bateman, A. & Fonagy, P. (2007). *Mentaliseringsbaseret behandling af borderline personlighedsforstyrrelse – en praktisk guide*. København: Akademisk Forlag.

Bateman, A. & Fonagy, P. (2012). *Handbook of Mentalization in Mental Health Practice*. Washington, DC: American Psychiatric Publishing.

Bateman, A. & Fonagy, P. (2019). *Mentalizing in Mental Health Practice*. Second edition. Washington, DC: American Psychiatric Publishing.

Baron-Cohen, S. (1995). *Learning, Development, and Conceptual Change. Mindblindness: An Essay on Autism and Theory of Mind*. The MIT Press. https://mitpress.mit.edu/books/mindblindness

Björnör, A.S. (2016). *Mentalisering i familjen–Family System Test som ett sätt att mäta mentaliseringsnivån i familjen* [Nordisk Mentaliseringskonferens 2016]. Stockholm: Svenskt Forum för Mentalisering.

Black, C. (2001). *It Will Never Happen to Me! Children of Alcoholics: As Youngsters–Adolescents–Adults*. New York, NY: Ballantine Books.

Blaustein, M.E. & Kinniburgh, K.J. (2010). *Treating Traumatic Stress in Children and Adolescents–How to Foster Resilience Through Attachment, Regulation and Competency (ARC)*. New York, NY: Guilford Press.

Bowlby, J. (1969). *Attachment and Loss*. New York, NY: Basic Books.

Byrne, G. (2016). *Illuminating the "Child-in-Mind" – A Mentalization-Based Treatment Programme, with Parents Following Severe Child Abuse and Neglect* [3rd International Conference–Mentalization-Based Therapy, MBT]. Genève: Université de Genève.

Cabrera, N.J., Fitzgerald, H.E., Bradley, R.H. & Roggman, L. (2014). The ecology of father-child relationships–an expanded model. *Journal of Family Theory and Review*, 6(4): 336–354.

CDC.gov (2016). *Key Statistics from the National Survey of Family Growth*. https://www.cdc. gov/nchs/nsfg/key_statistics/s.htm

Cohen, J.A., Mannarino, A.P. & Deblinger, E. (2006). *Treating Trauma and Traumatic Grief in Children and Adolescents*. New York, NY: Guilford Press.

Cooper, A. & Redfern, S. (2015). *Reflective Parenting: A Guide to Understanding What's Going on in Your Child's Mind*. London: Routledge.

Csibra, G. (2010). Recognizing communicative intentions in infancy. *Mind & Language*, 25(2): 141–168.

Daubney, M. & Bateman, A. (2015). Mentalization-based therapy (MBT): An overview. *Australian Psychiatry*, 23(2): 132–135.

Egelund, M. (1998). *En forskel der gør en forskel*. København: Hans Reitzels Forlag.

Elvén, B.H. & Wiman, T. (2016). *Rabalder i børnefamilien*. København: Dansk Psykologisk Forlag.

Ensink, K., Bégin, M., Normandin, L. & Fonagy, P. (2016). Maternal and child reflective functioning in the context of child sexual abuse: Pathways to depression and externalising difficulties. *European Journal of Psychotraumatology*, 27(7): 30611.

Feldman, R. (2007). Maternal versus child risk and the development of parent-child and family relationships in five high-risk populations. *Development and Psychopathology*, 19(2): 293–312.

Finkelhor, D., Gelles, R.J., Hotaling, G.T. & Straus, M.A. (red.) (1983). *The Dark Side of Familes–Current Family Violence Research*. London: Sage Publications.

Foghsgaard, L. (2016). Professor: Berøring fylder hjernen med "krammehormoner". *Politiken*, 16, April.

Fonagy, P. (2008). A genuinely developmental theory of sexual enjoyment and its implications for psychoanalytic technique. *Journal of the American Psychoanalytic Association*, 56(1): 11–36.

Fonagy, P. & Allison, E. (2014). The role of mentalizing and epistemic trust in the therapeutic relationship. *Psychotherapy*, 51(3): 372–380.

Fonagy, P., Gergley, G., Jurist, E. & Target, M. (2007). *Affektregulering, mentalisering ogselvets udvikling*. København: Akademisk Forlag.

Fonagy, P., Luyten, P., Campbell, C. & Allison, L. (2014). *Epistemic Trust, Psychopathology and the Great Psychotherapy Debate* [web-artikel]. The Society for the Advancement of Psychotherapy.

Fonagy, P. & Target, M. (1996). Playing with reality: I. Theory of mind and the normal development of psychic reality. *International Journal of Psychoanalysis*, 77(2): 217–234.

Forster, M. (2014). *Fem gange mere kærlighed – forskning og praktiske råd om et velfungerende familieliv*. København: Dansk Psykologisk Forlag.

Foucault, M. (1994). *Viljen til viden*. København: Det lille Forlag.

French, R.P. & Raven, B. (1959). The bases of social power. I: D. Cartwright (red.) *Studies in Social Power*. Ann Arbor, MI: University of Michigan, Institute for Social Research.

Freud, S. (1917). *The History of the Psychoanalytic Movement*. Nervous and Mental Disease Monograph Series, 25. New York: Nervous and Mental Disease Pub. Co.

Friedman, M.J., Keane, T.M. & Resick, P.A. (2007). *Handbook of PTSD – Science and Practice*. New York, NY: The Guilford Press.

Gallese, V., Fadiga, L., Fogassi, L. & Rizzolatti, G. (1996). Action recognition in the premotor cortex. *Brain*, 119: 593–609.

Glasl, F. (1997). *Konfliktmanagement–Ein Handbuch für Führungskräfte, Beraterinnen und Berater.* Stuttgart: Verlag Freies Geistesleben.

Goldie, P. (2004). Emotion, reason, and virtue. I: D. Evans & P. Cruse (red.) *Emotion, Evolution, and Rationality.* New York, NY: Oxford University Press.

Gottman, J.M. (1999). *The Marriage Clinic.* New York, NY: W.W. Norton & Company.

Gray, P. (2013). *Free to Learn.* New York, NY: Basic Books.

Guldin, M. (2014). *Tab og sorg – en grundbog for professionelle.* København: Hans Reitzels Forlag.

Gunderson, E.A., Gripshover, S.J., Romero, C., Dweck, S., Goldin-Meadow, S. & Levine, S.C. (2013). Parent praise to 1- to 3-year-olds predicts children's motivational frameworks 5 years later. *Child Development,* 84(5): 1526–1541.

Hafstad, R. & Øvreeide, H. (2011). *Utviklingstøtte–Foreldrefokusert arbeid med barn.* Kristiansand: Høyskoleforlaget.

Hagelquist, J.Ø. (2012). *Mentalisering i mødet med udsatte børn.* København: Hans Reitzels Forlag.

Hagelquist, J.Ø. (2015). *Mentaliseringsguiden.* København: Hans Reitzels Forlag.

Hagelquist, J.Ø. & Skov, M.K. (2014). *Mentalisering i pædagogik og terapi.* København: Hans Reitzels Forlag.

Harari, Y.N. (2015). *Sapiens – en kort historie om menneskeheden.* København: Lindhart & Ringhof.

Hari, R., Henriksson, L., Malinen, S. & Parkkonen, L. (2015). Centrality of social interaction in human brain function. *Neuron,* 88(1): 181–193.

Hughes, A., Aldercotte, A. & Foley, S. (2017). Maternal mind-mindedness provides a buffer for pre-adolescents at risk for disruptive behavior. *Journal of Abnormal Child Psychology,* 45(2): 225–235.

Ilg, F. & Ames, L.B. (1967). *Barnets adfærd.* København: Forlaget Rhodos.

Kilpatrick, K.L. & Williams, L.M. (1997). Post-traumatic stress disorder in child witnesses to domestic violence. *American Journal of Orthopsychiatry,* 67(4): 639–644.

Koefoed, P. & Visholm, S. (2011). Følelser i organisationen – psykodynamiske perspektiver. I: T. Heinskov & S. Visholm (red.) *Psykodynamisk organisationspsykologiII – på arbejde under overfladerne.* København: Hans Reitzels Forlag.

Kolk, B.V.D. (2005). Developmental trauma disorder – towards a rational diagnosis for children with complex trauma histories. *Psychiatric Annals,* 35(5): 401–408.

Larsen, K.C. & van der Weele, J. (2011). Helping families from war to peace: Trauma-stabilizing principles for helpers, parents and children. *Today's Children Are Tomorrow's Parents* (special edition): 30–31.

Levine, P.A. & Kline, M. (2007). *Trauma Through a Child's Eyes.* Berkeley, CA: North Atlantic Books.

Mayo Clinic Staff. (2013). *Empty Nest Syndrome: Tips for Coping.* Mayo Clinic, 17 marts.

Minuchin, S. (1978). *Familier og familieterapi.* København: Socialpædagogisk Bibliotek, Munksgaard.

Omer, H. (2004). *Non-Violent Resistance.* Cambridge: Cambridge University Press.

Ostler, T., Bahar, O.S. & Jessee, A. (2010). Mentalization in children exposed to parental methamphetamine abuse – relations to children's mental health and behavioral outcomes. *Attachment & Human Development,* 12(3): 193–207.

Perry, B.D. & Szalavitz, M. (2011). *Drengen der voksede op som hund.* København: Hans Reitzels Forlag.

Potegal, M. & Davidson, R.J. (2003). Temper tantrums in young children: 1. Behavioral composition. *Journal of Developmental and Behavioral Pediatrics*, 24(3): 140–147.

Quervain, D.J-F. de, Fischbacher, U., Treyer, V., Schellhammer, M., Schnyder, U., Buck, A. & Fehr, E. (2004). The neural basis of altruistic punishment. *Science*, 304(5688): 1254–1258.

Rollnick, S. & Fabring, C.A. (2016). *Den motiverende samtale i praksis*. København: Hans Reitzels Forlag.

Rossouw, T. (2012). Self-harm and young people: Is MBT the answer? I: N. Midgely & I. Vrouva (red.) *Minding the Child: Mentalization-Based Interventions with Children, Young People and Their Families*. London: Routledge.

Sadler, L.S., Slade, A., Close, N., Webb, D.L., Simpson, T., Fennie, K. & Mayes, L.C. (2013). Minding the baby: Enhancing reflectiveness to improve early health and relationship outcomes in an interdisciplinary home-visiting program. *Infant Mental Health Journal*, 34(5).

Shore, A. (2003). *Affect Regulation and the Repair of the Self*. New York, NY: W.W. Norton & Company.

Siegel, D.J. (2002). *Sindets tilblivelse og udvikling – nye psykologiske perspektiver*. Aarhus: Forlaget Klim.

Siegel, D.J. (2013). *Brainstorm–the Power and Purpose of the Teenage Brain*. New York, NY: Tarcher Perigee.

Siegel, D.J. & Bryson, T.P. (2012). *The Whole-Brain Child*. New York, NY: Bantam Books.

Siegel, D.J. & Bryson, T.P. (2014). *No-Drama Discipline*. New York, NY: Bantam Books.

Siegel, D.J. & Hartzell, M. (2003). *Parenting from the Inside Out–How a Deeper Self-Understanding Can Help You Raise Children Who Thrive*. New York, NY: Penguin Putnam.

Simonsen, E. & Møhl, B. (2017). *Grundbog i psykiatri*. København: Hans Reitzels Forlag.

Skårderud, F. & Sommerfeldt, B. (2014). *Miljøterapibogen – mentalisering som holdning og handling*. København: Hans Reitzels Forlag.

Sperber, D., Clément, F., Heintz, C., Mascaro, O., Mercier, U., Origgi, G. & Wilson, D. (2010). Epistemic vigilance. *Mind & Language*, 24(4): 359–393.

Spitz, R.A. (1945). Hospitalism – a follow-up report on investigation described. *The Psychoanalytic Study of the Child*, 1(2): 113–117.

Spock, B. (1954). *Bogen om barnet*. København: Politikens Forlag.

Steele, H. & Steele, M. (2005). The construct of coherence as an indicator of attachment security in middle childhood: The friends and family interview. I: K. Kerns & R. Richardson (red.) *Attachment in Middle Childhood*. New York, NY: Guilford Press.

Stroebe, M. & Schut, H. (1999). The dual process model of coping with bereavement – rationale and description. *Death Studies*, 23(3): 197–224.

Sundhedsstyrelsen & Statens Serum Institut. (2015). *Alkoholstatistik 2015*. Nationale data. København: Sundhedsstyrelsen.

Tangney, J.P., Stuewig, J. & Mashek, D.J. (2007). Moral emotions and moral behavior. *Annual Review of Psychology*, 58: 345–372.

Thinmer, L. & Hagelquist, J.Ø. (2017). Geniscenesættelse – en selvskadende traumeefterreaktion. *Psyke & Logos*, 37(2).

Twemlow, S.W., Fonagy, P. & Frank, C. (2004). The role of the bystander in the social architecture of bullying and violence in schools and communities. *Annals of the New York Academy of Sciences*, Bind 1036, Hæfte 1, Side 215–232.

Vygotsky, L.S. (1962). *Thought and Language*. Cambridge, MA: The MIT Press.

Winnicott, D.W. (1971). *Playing and Reality*. London: Routledge.

Index

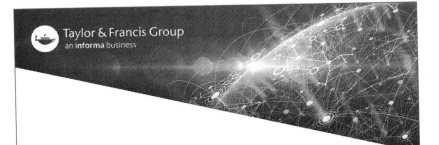

Printed in Great Britain
by Amazon

79633283R00160